Evil, Good, and Gender

Toronto Studies in Religion

Donald Wiebe
General Editor

Vol. 28

PETER LANG
New York • Washington, D.C./Baltimore • Bern
Frankfurt am Main • Berlin • Brussels • Vienna • Oxford

Jamsheed K. Choksy

Evil, Good, and Gender

Facets of the Feminine
in Zoroastrian Religious History

PETER LANG
New York • Washington, D.C./Baltimore • Bern
Frankfurt am Main • Berlin • Brussels • Vienna • Oxford

Library of Congress Cataloging-in-Publication Data

Choksy, Jamsheed K. (Jamsheed Kairshasp).
Evil, good, and gender: facets of the feminine
in Zoroastrian religious history / Jamsheed K. Choksy.
p. cm. (Toronto studies in religion; vol. 28)
Includes bibliographical references and index.
1. Zoroastrianism. 2. Women—Religious aspects—Zoroastrianism.
3. Good and evil. I. Title. II. Series.
BL1571 .C46   295'.178344—dc21   2001029563
ISBN 0-8204-5664-0
ISSN 8756-7385

Die Deutsche Bibliothek-CIP-Einheitsaufnahme

Choksy, Jamsheed Kairshasp:
Evil, good, and gender: facets of the feminine
in Zoroastrian religious history / Jamsheed K. Choksy.
−New York; Washington, D.C./Baltimore; Bern;
Frankfurt am Main; Berlin; Brussels; Vienna; Oxford: Lang.
(Toronto studies in religion; Vol. 28)
ISBN 0-8204-5664-0

The paper in this book meets the guidelines for permanence and durability
of the Committee on Production Guidelines for Book Longevity
of the Council of Library Resources.

© 2002 Jamsheed K. Choksy

All rights reserved.
Reprint or reproduction, even partially, in all forms such as microfilm,
xerography, microfiche, microcard, and offset strictly prohibited.

Printed in the United States of America

for CAROL
who dispels all the myths

Contents

List of Illustrations · ix

Preface and Acknowledgments · xi

ONE · *Introduction: Gender, Sanctity, and Demonology* · 1

TWO · *Dualism and the Feminine* · 9

THREE · *Deceit, Discord, Sexuality, and Avidity* · 31

FOUR · *Weakness, Imperfection, and Death* · 51

FIVE · *Society in Antiquity and the Middle Ages* · 75

SIX · *Conclusion: Modernity and Change* · 105

Notes · 121

Bibliography · 133

Index · 161

Illustrations

ONE · *Sasanian silver coin images of Anahita* · 47

TWO · *Temptation of Mashya and Mashyana* · 53

THREE · *Reward of female souls in heaven* · 66

FOUR · *Reward of male souls in heaven* · 67

FIVE · *Punishment of female souls in hell* · 69

SIX · *A male soul encounters its Daena* · 70

SEVEN · *Sasanian silver bowl images of Daenas* · 71

EIGHT · *Sasanian silver coin image of Boran* · 85

NINE · *Sasanian silver-gilt ewer with female images* · 89

Preface & Acknowledgments

The gestation of this volume has spanned many years. The materials it covers have proved both rich and challenging, their investigation involving a range of disciplines and a variety of languages from which I have translated passages. It is my hope that this book will stimulate further discussion of continuity and change in the history of religions generally and the history and historicity of Mazdaism or Zoroastrianism specifically.

My analyses have benefited from assistance, comments, and suggestions—both great and small—by Lois Beck, Jorunn Buckley, Heidi Burns, Carol Choksy, Khursheed Choksy, William Darrow, Richard Frye, Khojeste Mistree, Guity Nashat, Meher Noshirwani, Kimberley Patton, Dagmar Riedel, James Russell, Gernot Windfuhr, and Ehsan Yarshater. I am profoundly grateful to them for their insights, while accepting sole responsibility for the conclusions reached. Students in the classes on Gender, Religion, and History: Images of Women in Christian, Jewish, Muslim, and Zoroastrian Cultures, which I taught at Stanford University and Indiana University, are owed thanks for many stimulating discussions. Finally, my appreciation goes to Donald Wiebe for including this book in the series of which he is the general editor.

Fellowships from the American Academy of Religion, John Simon Guggenheim Memorial Foundation, and Andrew W. Mellon Foundation partially funded the research. Chapters of this book were presented as papers at the American Academy of Religion, the Center for the Study of World Religions at Harvard University, and the

Second Irano-Judaica Conference organized by the Hebrew University and the Ben-Zvi Institute. The book was finalized within the exceptionally pleasant setting of the Center for Advanced Study in the Behavioral Sciences at Stanford University. To all those institutions, I am in debt.

CHAPTER ONE

Introduction: Gender, Sanctity, & Demonology

Evil and good, as interlinked religious concepts, represent discourse in historical and socioreligious contexts on the nature of human morality, behavior, and suffering. Evil, in particular, becomes simultaneously the source and the explanation of individual unhappiness and communal plight. Associated with mystery, magic, shadows, darkness, night, and often, knowledge but not wisdom, evil has long been regarded as an invidious force that seeks to undermine society and disrupt the lives of individuals. Its origin is frequently attributed to a non-human spiritual being, with ancillary spirits and mortals acting as evil's agents—all in opposition to a spiritual entity who supposedly represents order and good. Different societies have reached divergent religious resolutions in attempts to explain the phenomenon of evil in their history and value systems. Nevertheless, since evil is usually apprehended as an abstraction by humans, it reflects a human worldview complete with aspects of sin, deceit, sex, impurity, and, very often, gender. Mazda-worship or Mazdaism, commonly called Zoroastrianism, and that faith's adherents, came over the centuries to postulate a concept of primordial, tangible, absolute evil whose "heart of darkness" lay in imperfection believed to originate from a distinct and flawed spiritual being, with a pandemonium of evil spirits as the instruments of defectiveness—even though the faith's doctrines did not begin that way. In time, an increasingly dualist Iranian theodicy fully equated evil to imperfection and endowed it with great power and independence, separate from all notions of the good, encompassing both moral and descriptive harm, human and cosmic wrongdoing. Dogma came to dictate that there could be no compromise with such evil. Radical evil within the religious experience could not be condoned, it was believed by the Middle Ages; evil had to be opposed by good. So, good and evil, like masculine and feminine, became vital categories that structured Zoroastrian spirituality through the writings of an all-male priesthood that has served the faith for most of its historical existence—just as similar categories did in other faiths (compare Lakoff 1987).

The notion that the feminine—including many aspects of the female and of women—was believed to be more chaotic, dangerous, evil, and, consequently, distant from the order and goodness of god became, I will suggest in this book, a perspective of the Mazdean or Zoroastrian religion for much of its history. This was not a mere inconsistency nor an occasional negative view (contra Boyce 1989: 308 note 83; de Jong 1995: 41). Granted, ancient and medieval clergy probably did not engage in introspective self-questioning on gender-related theoretical issues in the same manner that persons now do. Yet, gender has long been a crucial variable in religious belief even though its academic study is a recent development (Buchanan 1987: 443). The historical development of Zoroastrian concepts of good and evil when linked to the feminine, to the female, and to women by generations of clerics yielded demonic female spirits thought to personify undesirable characteristics. Attribution of cause and blame for those features to the feminine, as an agent of disorder, provided a means of locating them in the religious cosmos. The chaotic evil thought to be within humans thus came to be externalized in harmful spirits, particularly female demons, with a view to eventually contain and overcome it within a linear universal scheme of ecclesiastic historiography.

Many female demons inhabited the religious universe construed by the male priests and male theologians of the canonical Zoroastrianism or Mazda-worship that developed from the ancient period or antiquity (ca. 1750 B.C.E.–500 C.E., with late antiquity ca. 200–500 C.E.) to the medieval period or Middle Ages (ca. 500–1500 C.E.). Belief in some demonesses has even survived into the premodern and modern periods or contemporary times (ca. 1500 C.E.–present).[1] The evil supposedly embodied in Zoroastrian demonesses, as will be discussed, was never regarded as an ambivalent power: it was believed to be the very opposite of good. However, this does not imply that radical evil is exclusively feminine in either nature or origin. Indeed it is not, according to Mazdean cosmogony. Nor is the feminine excluded from goodness. Several female spiritual beings play important roles in Zoroastrian beliefs and rites, as also will be discussed, to repel evil and enhance good. Mortal women came to be expected to emulate, whenever and wherever possible, their divine spiritual counterparts. The functions of beneficial feminine entities—both in belief and as role models—would become especially important as counterbalances to the evil that Mazdeans feared, I suggest in this study.

The concept of gender appears fundamental to relationships within cultures and is based on perceived sexual differences (Buchanan 1987: 434). Yet, the term gender is not a substitute for woman, nor does it merely indicate relationships between the sexes. It is now regarded, at least in part, as a culturally-constructed idea that highlights definitions of the feminine, the female, and women in contrast to the masculine, the male, and men that have become entrenched in many societies around the world (Van Herik 1985: 15–16, 97, 115; Bynum 1986a: 7, 12).[2] Likewise, the term denotes sex-based inequalities in influence and power related to the dynamics of social authority (Bynum 1986a: 1–2; Scott 1988: 29–32, 42; 1991: 796). Earliest Mazdean tradition recognized the existence of gender differences (compare Windfuhr 1976: 273). Although ancient and medieval Mazda-worshipers did not directly grapple with gender theory, gender-specific issues did become central considerations in beliefs, practices, and attitudes. The impact of gender differences was felt within Zoroastrian communities—most particularly on socioreligious topics. In modern times, on the other hand, even theoretical questions relating to gender have been propelled to the foreground of societal change by a variety of factors including women's enhanced access to educational and economic resources plus increased intercultural contact.

The genesis of earliest Mazdean beliefs is shrouded in uncertainty. Many details might never be known beyond conjecture. Whatever its exact liturgical, ritualistic, and narrative origins may or may not have been, Mazdaism did develop rapidly into a devotional, religious tradition. The notions expressed in the earliest stratum of liturgies—as reflected in the Old Avestan corpus—established a doctrinal kernel from which later Mazdean theology and rites could be elaborated over the centuries (compare especially Windfuhr 1976: 269, 305–306; see also Kellens 2000: 112). That overall tradition is analyzed in this study. So, the present book examines doctrinal, theological, ritual, and socioreligious developments over time in the relationship between evil, good, and gender—within a context of malevolence and benevolence attributed to the feminine, the masculine, the female, and the male by Zoroastrians. It analyzes the impact of dualism, which was developed from nascent ideas that were extended in directions the earliest followers may not have conceived fully—serving as a major "unifying and organizing principle that holds the individual phenomena together" (Wach 1988: 38)—on the religion's attitudes toward gender-related issues. Elucidation of the gender-specific consequences of notions like order, piety, chastity, perfection, and purity, in contrast to notions of chaos, impiety, sexuality, imperfection, and pollution, is sought—not an apologia (Luhrmann 1996: 227). This book's chapters also involve probing the faith's extension of such concepts to encompass female spiritual beings and legendary figures in contrast to male spiritual beings and legendary protagonists. It then investigates the effect of belief and praxis on the lives of women in past and present Mazdean communities.

Essentially, this study explores implications of the feminine and masculine in religion—where doctrine was employed to produce a bifurcation based on gender—and suggests that images of the female and male in theology were fundamental in defining both women's and men's cultural roles and statuses (compare Buchanan 1987: 435). As such, the work focuses for the most part on the historical and historiographical—both diachronically and synchronically—development, impact, and transformation of beliefs, attitudes, and experiences within a religious tradition that still flourishes and is constantly undergoing transformation (compare James 1961/1974: 28–29, 48–49, 376–377; Wach 1988: 19, 56, 96, 160–161; Waardenburg 1999: vi, xvii). It describes and interprets seemingly rational and nonrational trends that produced a character distinct to the Zoroastrian faith and its practitioners, a development with monumental cultural consequences (see generally Durkheim 1912/1957: 29–37, 47, 409; James 1961/1974: 59, 62; Wach 1988: 26, 36, 49). Secular images of the feminine, female, and women as reflected through literature and art, plus the status of women in Zoroastrian societies past and present are discussed in direct connection with the religion.[3] The analytical survey which comprises this book is not intended to provide every iota of data. Readers are guided to specific primary sources and to additional, specialized, scholarly studies on individual issues through the references, notes, and bibliography.

While utilizing theoretical paradigms drawn from a range of disciplines—including anthropology, gender studies, historiography, history, linguistics, literary criticism, psychology, religious studies, and sociology—this study is firmly grounded in the source materials that Zoroastrianism provides. Most of the texts, artworks, and other items discussed herein possess both historiographic and literary facets, in addition to the more obvious religious and secular dimensions. Many also once had or still have didactic roles. The source materials were created by Mazda-worshipers not for scholarly perusal, although some clearly resulted from intellectual curiosity and didactic needs, but to function as part of a self-contained socioreligious and religiohistoriographical system. Therefore, the faith's practitioners past and present must be seen as the makers of their own reality through attitudes and events. In other words, they provide both the experiences and the significance of those experiences (see in general Gossman 1990: 3, 242–243, 248–250, 288–289; Scott 1988: 28–50; 1991: 784–786; Toews 1987: 906).

At the same time it is important to remember, from the outset, that Zoroastrian scripture and exegesis—and the array of material items that were influenced by the faith—reflect male discourses, either directly or indirectly, on both theodicy and gender. The images of the feminine, the female, and women recorded in the faith's literature and material objects were codified or created and then propagated largely by men over many centuries (compare generally Brown 1988: 9–12; and essays in Kaufmann 1989). For all cultures, the predilections of each writer, craftsman, or interpreter and of his time period are ever present—woven into the discourse surrounding every item (Levinson 1989a: 2, 10; 1989b: 20, 22). In particular, as products of priests and theologians, the religion's preserved views on men and women and on gender-related constructs of good and evil, order and disorder, reflect male contouring of the parameters of both the masculine and the feminine—dualism was given dimensions which, sometimes, connected evil to the feminine and good to the masculine. Perhaps, as in western Christian societies of the Middle Ages, notions associated with gender were viewed differently by members of the two sexes (see also Bynum 1986b: 277). Women's own interpretations of the relationship between religion and gender, however, have not been preserved within or outside the faith's canon, other texts, and non-textual artifacts for much of the faith's history. It is unclear whether such accounts and items even existed until the nineteenth and twentieth centuries C.E. Only thereafter, would Zoroastrian women, exposed to western secular education and feminist ideas, begin recording their viewpoints in documents and objects.

One additional caveat is in order. Contemporary expectations and sensibilities of which roles the feminine and masculine, the female and male, women and men should play in religion specifically and in society generally have little bearing on what occurred in the past. Projection of current mores backward in time, with concomitant expectations of gender equivalence, does not further pertinent understanding of a culture's past. Rather, what seems to have taken place and why it took place are valuable in comprehending each group's religious history and current practices—irrespective of how the data may correlate with modern predilections. Instead of simply viewing gender-related issues of the past as misogynist, it may be more useful to approach these issues as differential factors based on gender. Those differences can yield a wealth of information on how beliefs structure believers' lives. Human thoughts, attitudes, and values are often focused on specific issues. They frequently reflect attempts at activities intended to ensure individual and, often, communal well-being. Differential aspects of gender that arose over time, described and analyzed in the subsequent chapters, should be approached as examples of how a specific religious culture—that of Mazdaism or Zoroastrianism—developed, flourished, and survives.

Although the feminine—as demoness and woman—was periodically regarded in Mazdean religious beliefs as a propagator of evil, the feminine is never the origin par excellence of all that is maleficent. It appears the implicit assumptions of society required that in Zoroastrianism, as in Judaism, Christianity, and Islam, the origin of evil be attributed to the masculine, be it god or devil (compare Boyce 1979: 19–26; Awn 1983: 18–40; J. B. Russell 1987: 26–27; 1988: 174–178, 252–253; Levenson 1988: 47–50). From a psychoanalytical viewpoint, it seems that representation of the godhead as masculine in belief, narrative, and image reflects man's desire for paternal protection, and, by extension, the supreme source of harm must also be masculine (Van Herik 1985: 18). Such views of good and evil are both masculine and male because they exploit gender to establish and maintain a system which vests power in men. Those views often condemn the feminine and female as important agents of diabology while creating feminine and female divine images that are secondary to the masculine god and unattainable as symbols to female devotees.

It may be tempting to dismiss the beliefs, praxes, and stories that seem to differentiate between masculine and feminine, male and female, men and women in Zoroastrianism—and other religions—as outdated myths. But it is useful to remember that even myths served, and still serve, as a means of making a range of experiences meaningful to humans. Meaning comes to be endowed, in such cases, by relating experiences to culturally specific and societally significant issues, then preserving and transmitting the results across regions and eras to ensure that human actions are shaped or reshaped (compare Kirk 1973: 282; Doty 1986: 14, 16–19, 30–31). Even if merely part of a mythology, a society's doctrines, theologies, rituals, stories, and artifacts are linked to attempts at creating structure, order, and significance so that people can better understand and function within space and time. Whether viewed as myth or belief, the ideas generated and applied by faith to human actions also served to connect a poorly known, mythic, past through a progressive series of events to each person's present within a socioreligious scheme of communal history and historiography (compare Lévi-Strauss 1979: 11–13, 23, 38, 40–43). Thus, beliefs, praxes, and stories do reflect specific human preoccupations—such as those among the Mazda-worshipers with their concepts of good and evil—despite the variety and complexity of possible interpretations (see in general Kirk 1973: 9–31, 252–257).

Doctrines, rites, devout tales, art, and artifacts come to perform explanatory, validatory, and operative roles—positioning the faithful in a religiously-constructed scheme that endowed meaning upon human life in relation to other living creatures and the world as a whole over time (Doty 1986: 43–49). There are overlaps, especially in generalized aspects of attitudes toward the feminine, female, and women vis-à-vis the masculine, male, and men, between Zoroastrianism and other religions with which it interacted in the Near East and South Asia. But, for the most part, the details and developments were particular to Zoroastrians due to the nature of cultural relativity that differentiates at various levels between sectarian societies (compare Lévy-Bruhl 1926/1985; Boaz 1940). The religious concepts and narratives that developed within Mazdaism formed an interpretive system that bound devotees together across space and time through symbolism, rites, objects, and attitudes.[4] That system constantly connected and shaped issues of gender in terms of the religion's history and in terms of its historical representations by devotees.

CHAPTER TWO

Dualism & the Feminine

Zoroastrianism, a faith that eventually came to trace its tenets to words attributed by later tradition to an eponymous individual named Zarathushtra, and after whom it is now called, developed into a major religion in ancient and medieval Iran. During that period it influenced Hellenistic, Jewish, Christian, and Muslim beliefs. After the Arab Muslim conquest of Iran in the seventh to eighth centuries C.E., Zoroastrianism gradually lost adherents through conversion to Islam. Yet, Zoroastrian communities have endured not only in Iran, but also in India where they are called the Parsis (Parsees), "Persians," and in several other countries around the world. Zoroastrian (Zarathoshti, Zartoshti, Zardoshti) men and women often refer to themselves as Mazdayasna (Mazdesn), namely, Mazdeans or worshipers of Mazda, a term that acknowledges their veneration of the god Ahura Mazda or Ohrmazd.

The time, locale, life, and even the historicity of Zarathushtra (Zarduxsht, Zaratosht, Zardosht) have been the subject of much academic debate for decades with limited consensus. Generally, scholars have concluded that the time and place when he preached may range from the first millennium B.C.E. on the Iranian plateau to the second millennium B.C.E. on the Eurasian steppe (see Jackson 1899; Nyberg 1938/1966; Herzfeld 1947; Henning 1951; Burrow 1973; Shahbazi 1977; Eduljee 1980; Gnoli 1980, 1989; Dandamayev and Lukonin 1989; Boyce 1989, 1992; Gershevitch 1995). Other scholars have suggested much that survives about Zarathushtra is a myth (see Darmesteter 1892–1893; Molé 1963, 1967; Skjærvø 1996; Kellens 2000). The founder's persona may be ephemeral, but the texts attributed to him are not. Words ascribed to Zarathushtra provide a conceptualization of the socioreligious universe within which the ancient Iranians believed that they dwelled. Those words also provide, at the very least, the basic, innovative, ethical and ritual concepts that would permeate Zoroastrianism in later centuries (compare Windfuhr 1976: 269; 1996: 237–240; 1999: 295–296). A confluence of recent archeological and linguistic evidence now indicates that images apparently relating to Zarathushtra's lifetime can be ascribed to a period some time between the eighteenth and sixteenth centuries B.C.E. His homeland, based on words attributed to him, may have been somewhere in the region stretching from the Aral Sea eastward to Lake Balkhash and southward to Afghanistan and Baluchistan, i.e., the western and southern regions of present-day Central Asia (see additionally Eduljee 1980; J. R. Russell 1996). The society in which he composed might have been part of the Central Asian Bronze Age. Perhaps it was the Bactrian-Margiana Archeological Complex (ca. 2000–1750 B.C.E.). But, more likely, Zarathushtra's time coincided with the late Bronze Age period that witnessed a slow urban decline and a resurgence of pastoral nomadism—turbulence mentioned in the words attributed to him— a time which can be designated as the Post-Bactrian-Margiana Archeological Complex (ca. 1750–1500 B.C.E.) by modern scholars (see generally Lamberg-Karlovsky forthcoming; see specifically Sarianidi 1998: 168–175; Windfuhr 1999: 309–313; and Choksy forthcoming). His given name, Zarath-ushtra, is a compound word possibly meaning "[possessor of] old camels." The form Zoroaster, by which he is identified in western literature, was derived later from the ancient Greek rendering Zoroastres, after the Iranians had migrated on to the Near Eastern plateau that came to be named for them—by being called Iran—around the middle to end of the second millennium B.C.E.[1]

According to an extant hagiographic tradition that may originally have been distinct from the faith, Zarathushtra supposedly left home at the age of twenty. After a decade of wandering and contemplation, he is said to have received revelation and returned to preach the religion of Ahura Mazda who is worshipped as the supreme deity of Mazdaism or Zoroastrianism. Zarathushtra supposedly was opposed by the male clergy of the older cults in his native region. So he allegedly had to seek refuge at the court of a neighboring kavi (a term which, although often translated as "lord, chieftain," may have had a ritualistic function) named Vishtaspa who accepted the new religion. There, Zarathushtra preached and gained many followers—male and female, adults and children—until he was assassinated by a priest of another sect at the age of seventy-seven, or so it was written long after his lifetime. The sacred biography, occasionally called the Zarduxsht namag or Zardosht nama, "Book of Zarathushtra," that gradually developed around the persona of Zarathushtra was clearly influenced first by Indo-European notions of the holy man known to the early Iranians and later by biblical images of prophetic character after the Iranians had settled in the Near East (compare Molé 1963: 271–386). Traces of the past were recast and endowed with significance to create an image of how Zarathushtra's life should have transpired, at least according to pious historiography. Allusions and echoes, in part, help locate an individual life that was deemed to be important within a modified framework (compare generally M. Butler 1989: 83; Clark 1998: 19–21).

Despite what eventually came to be recorded as hagiography, and rather than viewing himself as a prophet, Zarathushtra may have seen his role as that of a devotional poet (Yasna 30: 1, 35: 2; contra among others Jackson 1899; Henning 1951; Weber 1956/1978; Boyce 1979, 1989, 1992). In this role, he would have been continuing then long-standing Indo-European and Indo-Iranian traditions of praising order and certain spiritual entities associated with it while casting blame for disorder upon other spiritual entities (Skjærvø 1996: 226–234; 1997: 104–108). It is clear that Zarathushtra was acknowledged as ritually knowledgeable, learned in sacred words, and possessing unique insight into a spirituality which he transmitted to others (compare Kellens 2000: xv–xvi, 85–89). In that function, his activities would have been integral to the early social organization of the ancient Iranians.[2] As the chosen speaker of appropriate words linking the material and spiritual realms, he may indeed have been regarded as a communal, religious leader. Irrespective of when and where Zarathushtra lived, what he may or may not have recited, if he composed individually or with others, whether Vishtaspa was a patron or a relative, and how he viewed his own societal role and life, during the centuries that followed those words attributed to him became central to a set of religious tenets whose origins were traced back to him by the cohorts of an evolving devotional tradition. Moreover, the image of Zarathushtra gradually became so very important within that emergent tradition that, eventually, the notion of his existence came to serve as one of the basic nodes of a pious historiography (Malandra 1996: 139). In time, the nascent sect or sects whose members repeated Zarathushtra's words—which they believed to be prophetic ones—came to be associated with a clerical group.

Herodotus (ca. 484–430 B.C.E.), the early Greek historian, mentioned that no ancient Iranian religious rite could be performed without the presence of a male priest—a magu-paiti, makush, perhaps magavan, mowbed, mowmard, or magus (I: 101, 132). He also listed practices specific to the magi, such as the exposure of corpses to wild creatures (I: 140). The magi, originally a priestly group among an Iranian tribe called the Medes, seem to have adopted the ideas attributed to Zarathushtra after those concepts had begun to spread among the ancient Iranians, serving as clerics of the sect (see Weber 1956/1978: I, 501; Cook 1983: 155; Schwartz 1985: 696–697; Dandamayev and Lukonin 1989: 331–333). It is interesting to note, in terms of social and gender issues, that ecclesiastic membership among the magi, as opposed to their familial ties, never included women. Through contact with the magi, Greek and Roman authors learned of Zarathushtra. For Hellenistic scholars, particularly the followers of Pythagoras, Zarathushtra became a mystical figure and the chief of magicians—a term deriving from the Old Iranian word magu-paiti borrowed into Greek as mágos and Latin as magus. In time, the magi claimed that Zarathushtra had been a member of their group—turning the image of the traditional, devotional, poet into that of a historical, prophetic, leader whose ministering they represented themselves as continuing. Magian claims proved to be highly effective, for by the fourth century B.C.E. even the Greek philosopher Plato (ca. 427–347 B.C.E.) referred to Zoroaster as a magus (I: 121). Over the centuries that followed, Zoroastrian (and especially magian) tradition firmly grounded itself on the belief that Zarathushtra had preached a religion. In this process of reformulating Zarathushtra's image, the magi also may have begun to assume the theological roles that some of them clearly engaged in by late antiquity and the Middle Ages.

Through this process of assimilation and transformation, Zarathushtra became a sage and the founder of the Iranian religion—perhaps posthumously. Belief that devotional poetry whose composition was attributed to him contained spiritual revelation from a divine being called Ahura Mazda came to be accepted as central to the religiosity of ancient and medieval Iranians (compare Yasna 29: 8). For numerous persons over many successive generations—past and present—Zarathushtra was the prophet who founded the Mazdayasna religion, and faith in that belief shaped or shapes their thoughts, actions, and lives. The magi themselves were introduced into Christian belief as the wise men from the east who supposedly journeyed to Bethlehem—thus linking Zoroastrianism to yet another Near Eastern faith. The contemporary priesthood, whose members are called mobeds, traces its lineage to the ancient magi of Iran. Passed from father to son, but in no clearly documented cases to a daughter, priesthood involves long years of studying the liturgies and rituals of Zoroastrianism, starting during childhood. This is followed by formal initiation as a priest via a two-stage ritual process now involving the Navar (Nawar) and Martab (Maratib) ceremonies in India (Kotwal 1988).

The Zoroastrian scripture is known as the Abestag or Avesta (probably from Upa-Stavaka), possibly meaning "Praise" (Kellens 1989: 36). The Avesta includes the Gathas (Gah), "Devotional or Reverential Poems, Songs," believed to have been composed by the devotional poet Zarathusthra himself, in which his name as versifier and worshiper is mentioned both directly and indirectly, and through which his ideas were conveyed (Schwartz 1986, 1991). The basic parameters within which devotionalism would develop during the centuries that followed can be glimpsed in those verses. The Gathas seem to have been transmitted orally by athravans (atravaxshes) or "fire priests," zaotars or "libation offerers," magi, and lay men and women who adopted Zarathushtra's words, for centuries, with some variations and additions. The Avesta also includes the Yasna

Haptanghaiti, "Worship in Seven Chapters," which like the Gathas was composed in Old or Gathic Avestan probably by early acolytes of Zarathushtra or by a related sect of Mazdean thought (Narten 1986; Humbach and Ichaporia 1994: 14; Kellens 2000: 39–40, 94). The Yashts, "Devotional Poems [to Divine Beings]," in honor of spiritual entities whose praise was assimilated into the sect from earlier Iranian veneration, and the Videvdad (Widewdad) or Wendidad, "Code to Ward-off Evil Spirits," all in Young (Younger) or Standard Avestan, comprise yet other sections of the scripture that were composed between the sixth century B.C.E. and the fifth century C.E. (compare Kellens 2000: 35–37, 100). Between the fifth and seventh centuries C.E., during the Sasanian era, the Avesta finally was codified into a text from which its extant versions derive (Boyce 1968a: 33–36; Hoffman 1970: 188; Kellens 1996a, 2000: 2, 32–34, 38). Devotional poems that gained the status of prayers—such as the Ashem Vohu, "Righteousness is Good," (Yasna 27: 14), and the Ahuna Vairya (Ahunawar) or Yatha Ahu Vairyo, "As is the Lord," (Yasna 27: 13), both of which were composed in Old Avestan—and, thus, came to be recited in daily religious observances were also gathered together into the Xwurdag Abestag or Khorde Avesta, "Shorter Avesta."

Next in importance are texts clearly intended to serve as religious exegeses written in Pahlavi, a Middle Iranian language. Among the fairly extensive Pahlavi literature is the Zand or "Exegetical Commentary" on the Avesta. The Arda Wiraz namag, "Book of the Righteous Wiraz," preserves the description of a mythical voyage through heaven, limbo, and hell. It, together with other Zoroastrian accounts of the afterlife, seems to have influenced the Isra', "Night Journey," and Mi'raj, "Ascent," cycles attributed to the prophet Muhammad (ca. 570–632 C.E.) in Muslim tradition. Accounts of Muhammad's journey, in turn, may eventually have provided the basis for Dante's Divine Comedy. Indeed, Dante's (1265–1321 C.E.) introduction of limbo and his use of ice as the punishment in deepest hell, although at variance with the Christian tradition of his time, were well-known in Zoroastrian eschatology. The Denkard, "Acts of the Religion," another ninth-century C.E. Pahlavi codex, is an encyclopedic collection of the wisdom of medieval magi. Finally, there is more recent Zoroastrian religious literature in the New Persian and Gujarati languages—such as the Persian Revayats, "Persian Treatises," and the Rehbar-e Din-e Jarthushti, "Guide to the Zoroastrian Religion," respectively. These texts continued to transmit, to lay male and female believers who no longer understand the Avestan or Pahlavi languages, tenets of the religion and the meanings of rituals. Descriptions of the religion are now available in English, as well, for devotees of the faith.[3]

Zarathushtra appears to have differentiated, in the devotional poems of praise and blame attributed to him, between a neuter Asha, "order, reality" which was equated to "righteousness," and a feminine Drug, "disorder, illusion" which was equated to "falsehood." Thereby, he seems to have been evoking a rudimentary dualism which had ritual implications in addition to social ones. This nascent dualism was personified by Zarathushtra, it seems, in a pair of primal spirits: Mazda Ahura (later Avestan Ahura Mazda, Old Persian Auramazda, Assyrian Assara Mazas, Pahlavi Ohrmazd), the wise lord or deity of wisdom—initially via a creative hypostasis called Spanta Manyu or Spenta Mainyu, the beneficent mentality or spirit—and Angra Mainyu (Pahlavi Ahreman), the evil mentality or spirit.[4] To persons like Zarathushtra, these two entities were "the holier one ... and the evil one," or "the better and the worse" respectively (Yasna 45: 2, 30: 3–11). Ahura Mazda appears to have been regarded as the divinity of the "radiant sky," as the "father of order," and as the "creator of all these [beneficial] things" (Yasna 36: 6, 44: 3, 7). However, the Gathas are not systematically dualistic in content (compare Kellens 2000: 14). Rather the verses therein acknowledge a constant tension between the forces of order and chaos in a ritualistic universe which is bounded by cosmogony and eschatology (contra Kellens 2000: 3–4, 17). So it was thought that in existence—as through correctly performed rituals—people and deities could bind themselves firmly to Asha, thereby symbolically ordering the cosmos in an enlightened fashion (see further Kuiper 1964; Kellens 2000: 65, 75). Only later on did doctrinal modifications, by generations of magi, transform the devotional poet's dualistic words into a cosmic duality—at the latest by the sixth century C.E. (see Weber 1956/1978: I, 523; Choksy 1996: 100–104). Thus Angra Mainyu, originally the primary opponent of Spenta Mainyu, clearly stands in opposition to Ahura Mazda within medieval theology (Duchesne-Guillemin 1985a: 670). The established or orthodox version of Zoroastrianism then came to rigorously follow a dualism between righteousness and evil on a universal scale—not withstanding a heterodox variant that attempted to bridge the duality by ascribing both spirits to the shortcomings of Zurvan "Time" (on which see Zaehner 1972).

As the devotional tradition was augmented slowly after Zarathushtra's lifetime it also came to be believed that the wise lord, through Spenta Mainyu, had created six specific Amesha Spentas or beneficent spiritual beings representing aspects of material creation: Vohu Manah or Wahman, "Good Thought," (animals); Asha Vahishta or Ardwahisht, "Best Righteousness," (fire); Xshathra Vairya or Shahrewar, "Power, Desirable Dominion," (metal); Spenta Armaiti or Spendarmad, "Good Disposition," later "Holy Devotion," (earth); Haurvatat or Hordad, "Integrity, Wholeness," later "Perfection," (water); and Ameretat or Amurdad, "Immortality," (plants). In the Gathas, Zarathushtra did not refer consistently to a specific list of holy immortals nor to any particular fixed ranking among them (compare Lommel 1930: 24–88; Narten 1982: 1–10; Kellens and Pirart 1988: I, 27–29; Humbach 1991: I, 14; Kellens 2000: 14, 50, 61–62). Yet, his words established the basis for this category of spirits (compare recently Windfuhr 1996: 240–241). His words in one passage of the Gathas (Yasna 47: 1) also may have provided the basic outline of their internal hierarchy. As a result, a category of spiritual entities collectively called Spenta Amesha did develop in the Old Avestan devotional poetry of the Yasna Haptanghaiti (39: 3). Then, within the Young or Standard Avestan texts, in the form of Amesha Spentas these spiritual beings came to represent a multivalent, hierarchical, gender-based, symbolic division of the religious universe into three active masculine and neuter domains paired with three passive feminine domains (compare Duchesne-Guillemin 1966: 31–39; Narten 1982: 98–102; Kellens 2000: 21, 48–49, 52–53). More specifically, those entities were not simply paired but manipulated to form a triple matrix having ethical and spiritual parameters with varying degrees of simplicity and complexity, tangibility and abstraction (see insights by Windfuhr 1996: especially 237, 241–250). After incorporation of the Yashts into the devotional tradition of the descendents of Zarathushtra's early followers, it was said that Ahura Mazda had created still more spirits. These included minor male and female Yazatas or Yazads, "praiseworthy spiritual entities," like Mithra or Mihr (signifying agreements, friendship, and sunlight) and Anahita or Anahid (representing fluids, fertility, and transmission of authority)—again displaying a symbolic, interlinked, gender-based, division into active masculine and passive feminine entities having both moral and cosmic features—to assist in protecting the material creations.

It was thought that, in response, Angra Mainyu supposedly had produced numerous Daevas or Dews, Indo-Iranian "divine entities" who came to be abjured as "demons" and "demonesses," including those causing avarice like Azi or Az, pollution like the demoness Nasush or Nas, and death like the demon of bones Asto Vidhatu or Astwihad, to attack the spiritual and material worlds. Essentially, spiritual entities venerated by the earliest Iranians were assimilated into the emergent Mazdean faith and then assigned differential valence as either agents of order or disorder, with support of order regarded as good and support of disorder regarded as evil. It is important to note that, unlike in the gender-specific symbolical construction of the spiritual realm of goodness, there was far less division along gender-specific active and passive lines attributed to the spirits of the realm of evil. Moreover, rather than being able to create ex nihilo (*brehenidan, dadan*) like Ahura Mazda supposedly does, medieval magi felt that Angra Mainyu can generate (*kirrenidan*) his creations only through the corruption of existing good ones.

During the early modern period, the beliefs of Zoroastrians gradually changed, under the influences of Protestant Christianity and western social mores, from a dualism based on polytheistic or henotheistic pantheons and pandemoniums to a quasi-monotheism in which Ahura Mazda often is regarded as the sole god and Angra Mainyu has become the devil (compare Jackson 1903: 363). The minor divinities of the original pantheon now have been accorded a variety of positions, usually equivalent to angels. The creatures of the original pandemonium have become minor evil spirits and ghouls.

European missionaries played a pivotal role in this transformation of Parsi and, later, Iranian beliefs. Yet, even at present, most Mazdeans continue to believe that humans serve a vital function in the struggle between god and the devil, representing order or good versus chaos or evil respectively. Moreover, in recent decades there has been a trend back to dualist beliefs—while maintaining Ahura Mazda's supremacy over an assemblage of divine spirits as was the case initially in the Old Avesta—among the orthodox (Choksy 1996: 104).

The sectarian sacred history, which developed from a range of Indo-European and Indo-Iranian myths, was divided into two periods. Prior to the first period was eternity, it is believed, when the primordial entities Ahura Mazda and Angra Mainyu were separate from each other. The first period was that of creation, and it lasted six thousand years. The initial three thousand years of this period were marked by the first encounter between Ahura Mazda and Angra Mainyu, the genesis of beneficent and malevolent spiritual beings by the wise lord and the evil spirit respectively, and an offer of peaceful coexistence in purity and righteousness which was rejected by the evil spirit. After Angra Mainyu had spurned Ahura Mazda's overture of peace, he was temporarily defeated by that wise lord who chanted the Ahunawar prayer. On hearing these holy words the evil spirit is said to have collapsed, stupefied, back into the darkness. The next three thousand years passed while Angra Mainyu lay in a stupor, and Ahura Mazda transformed the spiritual creations into corporeal ones. According to religious lore preserved in a Pahlavi language, text titled the Bundahishn, "[Book of] Primal Creation," (1a: 1–21, 4: 10–28, 33: 1–27), Ahura Mazda fashioned the Earth inside the sphere of the sky. That sphere, supposedly made of stone, was thought to enclose the oceans, seven continents, and the firmament with the sun, moon, planets, and stars. On the central continent, Ahura Mazda placed the first human—an androgyne named Gayo-Maretan, "Mortal Life," the primordial bull, and the first plant. The first six-thousand-year period of creation was followed, it is believed, by the current age of mixture between good and evil which will also last six thousand years. Angra Mainyu was aroused from his stupor by a demoness, invaded the world, polluted it, and then slew Gayo-Maretan, the primordial bull, and the first plant with the demoness' assistance, according to this cosmogonical account. Owing to Ahura Mazda's intervention, humanity supposedly arose from the semen of the androgyne, animals and cereals from the body of the first bull, and other plants from the seed of the initial plant.

Human history passed by, in this scheme of religious history, with the rise and fall of legendary dynasties until Zarathushtra was born in the religious year 8,970. Thirty years later, Zarathushtra received revelation from Ahura Mazda and preached the wise lord's faith. According to this sacral history, the era of Zarathushtra was followed by those of the Achaemenians (550–330 B.C.E.), Parthians (247 B.C.E.–224 C.E.), and Sasanians (224–651 C.E.). Thereafter, the Arabs conquered Iran, and were succeeded by Turkish invaders. These conquests, triggering the reduction of Mazda-worship to a minor faith and Zoroastrians to the status of a religious minority, were incorporated into the faith's mythohistory and explained in terms of a steady increase in evil which allegedly heralds the eventual advent of the final days—or so it was written in the Zand i Wahman Yasn, "Commentary on the Hymn to Vohu Manah," an anonymous ninth-century C.E. apocalyptic text (3: 20–29). Thereafter, it is claimed, that time progressed onward to the present when Mazda-worship is not widely practiced and Zoroastrians are a minority around the world. It is important to note that, in the written versions of this religious time-scheme, women, female beings, and the feminine serve only very limited positive roles such as procreation. As will be discussed, many roles of the feminine in this devout, universal, history were deemed by the faithful to be negative ones at the spiritual and corporeal levels.

For devotees, the material world came to be viewed as not merely the arena in which humans combat evil. Zoroastrians regard it as the trap into which the evil spirit was lured. Once trapped in matter, Angra Mainyu ostensibly is gradually vanquished via good thoughts, good words, and good deeds by divine beings and devotees acting in unison—this became the faith's and each practitioner's raison d'être within the religious mindset (compare Weber 1956/1978: I, 462, 533, 579–580). A ninth-century C.E. text titled the Shkand Gumanig Wizar, "Doubt Dispelling Exposition," allegorically describes this belief by comparing Ahura Mazda to a wise gardener who protects his garden, which is a paradise, by luring an attacking animal into a trap (4: 63–80). The sphere of the sky supposedly serves as the fortification of this cosmic snare in which divine beings and humans battle evil. The rewards of heaven, after death, are offered to the souls of believers—but on gender-differential bases as will be discussed—who have upheld righteousness and combated evil during their lifetimes (Boyce 1979; Choksy 1989a).

Zoroastrians believe (Hadhoxt Nask 2: 1–3: 36) that when an individual dies, his or her *urvan*, "mortal soul," sits near the head of the corpse for three days and nights. Demons and demonesses prey upon the soul during this period, but are thought to be kept at bay by a fire which the deceased individual's relatives kindle. On the dawn of the forth day, Sraosha or Srosh, the divinity of observance and prayer, approaches the righteous soul, opposes the demonic spirits of death, and leads the soul to Chinvato-Peretu (Chinwad Puhl), "bridge of the builder" or "bridge of the compiler." Here the soul is greeted by its conscience in the form of a beautiful spiritual maiden or Daena (Den). Sraosha, however, does not approach the soul of a sinner. Such an impure soul is fettered by demonic creatures and led to the bridge where it is greeted by its conscience in the form of a hag (Dadestan i Denig 24: 5–6, 25: 4–5; Shkand Gumanig Wizar 4: 92–97). Each soul supposedly undergoes individual judgment, presided over by a triad of divine beings—Mithra the divinity overseeing covenants, Rashnu or Rashn the spiritual judge, and Sraosha who came to be viewed as a celestial messenger. If the soul's good deeds are greater than its evil deeds, these divine beings intercede on its behalf and save it from the demonic hordes. The pure soul is then led across the bridge into Garo-demana (Garodman) or Wahisht, i.e., heaven or paradise (from pairi-daeza), by its Daena and Sraosha. However, if the soul is unrighteous and its evil deeds outweigh all the good it did while alive, the impure soul is condemned, bound by the demons and demonesses, and then cast into Dushox, i.e., hell, to await the day of universal judgment. In those cases where a soul's good and evil deeds are equal, it supposedly is consigned to a state of limbo in Hamestagan, i.e., the place of parity, until the end of time. The Zoroastrian doctrine of heaven, hell, and limbo is an excellent example of a religious concept which influenced other faiths. Islam absorbed not only heaven, hell, and limbo, but the entire scheme involving individual judgment at a spiritual bridge and a paradise filled with beautiful, pliant, feminine spirits. Christianity also assimilated the Zoroastrian belief in the afterlife of souls.

The present years thought to be filled with evil, pollution, and suffering will, in established Zoroastrian belief, be followed by two millennia during which three male saviors will be born, one every thousand years, to purify the world. Finally, in the religious year 11,973, the last savior, Saoshyant or Soshans, would resurrect the dead. Thereafter, Ahura Mazda will descend to earth with the other divinities, and the last savior will separate the righteous human souls from the evil ones. Each sinner, having already suffered after death, will be purified of his or her transgressions and impurities by means of an ordeal involving molten metal. Immortality of body and soul supposedly will be granted to all humans. Ahura Mazda, the beneficent immortals, and other divine beings will then annihilate all the demons and demonesses. Angra Mainyu himself will be forced to scuttle back into hell. Finally, hell will be sealed shut with molten metal, safeguarding the spiritual and material worlds from evil forever—or so Zoroastrians believe. Once the separation of evil from good has been accomplished, Ahura Mazda would renovate the universe in the religious year 12,000. Human history will end, eternity would recommence in absolute perfection, and humanity should begin dwelling in happiness upon a refurbished earth according to Zoroastrian eschatological doctrine (Bundahishn 34: 1–32; Zand i Wahman Yasn 9: 1–23). It is clear that Indo-European and Indo-Iranian myths of creation and destruction came together in the composition of Zoroastrian eschatology.

Between the ages of seven and fifteen each Zoroastrian boy or girl undergoes initiation into the religion. The ceremony now is termed the Navjote, "new birth," or Sedra-Pushun (Sedra-Pushi), "donning the sacred undershirt," and it symbolizes a spiritual rebirth. Exactly when this ceremony began is unclear, although it appears to have been practiced by both genders since at least the Middle Ages. After initiation each believer becomes fully responsible for his or her own religious, moral, and communal life. During the ceremony, the initiate—having learned the basic prayers of the religion—dons a white undershirt called the *sudra*, *sedra*, or *shabi* (earlier *shabig*) and ties a sacred cord or girdle known as the *kusti* or *kushti* (earlier *aiwyanghana, kustig*) around the waist. The initiation ceremony is still regularly performed by Zoroastrians all over the world. The sacred girdle, which most Zoroastrians continue to wear, must be untied and retied with the recitation of prayers on awakening each morning and prior to performing worship at fire temples (Boyce 1977: 236–240; Choksy 1989a: 54–60).

Most Mazdean rituals now are conducted within complexes known as fire temples. Fire is regarded by Zoroastrians as one of seven sacred creations, the others being water, earth, metal, plants, animals, and humans. In addition, fire is believed to be capable of vanquishing evil through purity. Consequently, it became the icon of the Zoroastrian faith much like the cross is for Christianity. Mazdean rites may not always have been performed for the most part within buildings. Initially, many aspects of worship might have been done outdoors—as noted by Herodotus (I: 131–132). Outdoor fire altars were used in Achaemenian times, as evidenced both by archeological remains at Pasargadae and by tomb reliefs at Naqsh-e Rostam (Stronach 1978: 138–145, plates 103–107; Schmidt 1970: plates 19, 40–41, 48–49, 56–57). Yet, temples with ritual fires were also present in Iran and Central Asia even prior to that period (see recently Garrison 1999 with references to earlier studies). Later, in the Sasanian period for example, rites were conducted both outdoors and indoors in front of fire altars. After Zoroastrianism became a minority faith, however, most rites involving fire would have been moved indoors so as to prevent vitiation of the votive acts and desecration of the fires through the presence of nonbelievers. At present, a sacred fire is kept constantly burning in an altar at each of the major fire temples in India and in Iran. Smaller temples in Pakistan, Sri Lanka, the United States of America, Canada, and elsewhere often do not maintain sacred fires; but a fire is usually lit in an altar prior to acts of worship being performed. The central devotional ceremony performed in major fire temples is the Yasna (Yasn, Ijashne), "worship, sacrifice," ritual where, among other rites, the haoma plant (now ephedra) is pounded, mixed into a libation, and symbolically offered by the priest to Ahura Mazda and other divinities. At a lower level, Jashan, "thanksgiving," services may also be performed at fire temples on days such as Nav Ruz or the Spring festival and Mihragan or the Autumn festival, as are the Gahanbars or communal feasts. Women generally may not conduct rituals in fire temples—although a medieval, Pahlavi language, reference in the Nerangestan, "Ritual Code, Ritual Directions," compiled in extant form post-tenth century C.E. when the number of magi in Iran was declining under Muslim hegemony, suggests that women could do so if properly trained and not menstruating (I, 22: 2–5). Women, like laymen, can also participate as both observers and patrons of rituals when in a state of ritual purity, i.e., when not regarded as polluted by menses, childbirth, or contact with an unclean item (Boyce 1977: 99–107; Choksy 1989a: 78–107).

Zoroastrians or Mazda-worshipers now are perhaps best known to Europeans and Americans for their practice of exposing the dead to vultures and other wild creatures. As alluded to earlier, this practice appears to have been introduced by the ancient magi in order to prevent pollution of the sacred earth, fire, and water by corpses. Zoroastrian doctrine holds that earth, fire, and water are desecrated if pollution reaches those elements from a human corpse which is buried, cremated, or interred in water. Consequently, in ancient times corpses were "mangled by bird or dog ... [then] before the Persians bury the body in the earth they embalm it [the remains] in wax" (Herodotus I: 140). As the population increased, it probably became difficult to discretely expose the dead. So, in medieval and modern times the corpse would be washed, then carried to a daxma or funerary tower, and placed in gender and age specific areas for men, women, and children within a circular enclosure which is open to the sky. Once the corpse has been mangled by birds and desiccated by sunlight, the bones would be collected and placed in a repository or in a pit filled with lime at the center of the tower. Exposure of the dead for mangling is by no means unique to Mazdaism—it came to be practiced by many sects of Central Asian origin including Tibetan Lamaism—although Zoroastrians eventually constructed sites for this ritual purpose. A similar praxis may also have been brought to North America by the ancestors of the plains Indians.

The nineteenth and twentieth centuries C.E. witnessed considerable variation in Zoroastrian funerary practices. Exposure of corpses was gradually phased out in Iran during the 1960s. Iranian Zoroastrians now bury their dead, after washing the corpse and wrapping it in a white shroud. Parsi Zoroastrians in India and Pakistan continue the tradition of exposing bodies to vultures in funerary towers, particularly at the cities of Bombay (now called Mumbai) and Karachi were many Zoroastrians reside. However, in Sri Lanka (where, initially, exposure was attempted but given up as impractical in the urban setting of the city of Colombo), Australia, England, the United States of America, and Canada, and even in other locales of India and Pakistan, most Zoroastrians—like their Iranian coreligionists—inter the dead. Generally, the bodies are buried in separate graves, in rows, without any gender or age based distinctions. The return to burial marks a revival of pre-magian funerary praxis, for the earliest Zoroastrians seem to have interred the dead (Videvdad 3: 8, 12). Hence, the term *daxma* originally referred to a grave rather than to a funerary tower (Hoffman 1965: 238). Recently, some Zoroastrian communities, particularly in North America, have begun cremating their dead—disregarding the ritual stipulation that fire not be polluted—in an attempt to accommodate modern, urban, lifestyles.

After the Arab conquest of Iran in the seventh century C.E., conversion to Islam gradually occurred and reached its zenith by the ninth through twelfth centuries C.E. The Muslim authorities initially restricted conversion in order to maintain a steady revenue from the *jizya*, "poll tax," which was extracted from each non-Muslim, but later enforced the espousing of Islam. Reconversion back to Zoroastrianism by an apostate who had adopted Islam was possible, even if the person involved could not openly profess his or her Zoroastrian faith. However, in most cases, return to the faith appears to have been infrequent, and, after conversion to Islam occurred, even if the first generation of converts were not practicing Muslims, their offspring were usually raised within an Islamic society and lost contact with Zoroastrians. Women, in their role as maternal transmitters of tradition, played important roles within familial settings in this transition from a Zoroastrian to an Islamic socioreligious culture in medieval Iran. The threat of absorption into the increasingly large

Muslim community reinforced the Zoroastrian tendency toward cultural preservation, and as the community grew smaller this tendency increased. Finally, many Zoroastrians withdrew from all major forms of interaction with Muslims and sought refuge in the thinly populated regions of central Iran at cities like Yazd (Choksy 1997).

One means of avoiding Muslim overlordship was for Zoroastrians to emigrate. Some noble families and their retainers—including Sasanian princes such as Peroz the son of Yazdagird III (ruled 632–651 C.E.)—relocated to China via Central Asia. Their descendents survived there, even building fire temples, until the thirteenth century despite proscription in 845 C.E. (Pulleyblank 1992: 425–426, 429). Other groups moved to the Caucasus without much success (Frye 1975: 96). The Parsis or Indian Zoroastrians are the descendants of émigrés who migrated to the western coast of India, perhaps in the tenth century C.E., to escape sectarian persecution and to avoid conversion to Islam. Those immigrants gradually dispersed to towns and villages in the Gujarat province, becoming farmers, carpenters, weavers, and merchants. Most public roles were restricted largely to men, domestic functions reserved for women. Education was usually trade-related and generally available to sons, less often to daughters. Each male priest ministered to a few families. Over time, such associations become hereditary. Around 1290 C.E., those priests divided into five ecclesiastic groups. By the thirteenth century C.E., extensive contact between Parsi and Iranian Zoroastrians had recommenced with the Iranians eventually sending texts that would educate and guide the Parsis in religious matters. Pressure from Hindus compelled Parsis to make religious and social changes. Ritual sacrifice of bulls and cows was abandoned due to Hindu reverence for these animals. The Parsis came to be regarded as a caste within Hindu society; thus the religion became hereditary on the Indian subcontinent with no converts being accepted.

Contact between Parsis and Europeans began with the establishing of trading houses in the seventeenth century C.E. As trade increased, so did the wealth and size of the Parsi community. In 1661 C.E., the city of Bombay came under the administration of the British East India Company. There, Parsis grounded the community's fiscal success on shipbuilding and on the cotton and opium trade with China. Parsis also established themselves in textile manufacture, general commerce, and banking. The community became a mercantile arm of the British and controlled India's foreign trade for over two centuries. They adopted secular education from the British and promoted it by founding schools for their sons and daughters. Following mores that were emerging in Europe at the time, the Parsis began encouraging educated women to take up careers in public workplaces—as will be discussed in more detail in chapter six. They also funded hospitals and philanthropic trusts for the community. All these developments spurred relocation away from the villages to large cities—especially to Bombay. Thus, between the eighteenth and nineteenth centuries C.E., the Parsi Zoroastrians of India developed into an urbanized middle class. The community also helped found the industrial base of modern India. Parsi entrepreneurs established the iron and steel industries, hydroelectric plants, the Indian Institute of Science, and the Indian atomic energy research institute (see further Boyce 1979: 166–217).

Although international dispersion occurred for a variety of socioeconomic reasons during the 1950s to 1990s, Parsis still dwell in most major cities of India, particularly Bombay, Delhi, and Calcutta. The Parsi community presently numbers around 76,400 in India, 2,800 in Pakistan, approximately 10,000 in Canada and in the United States of America, 4,000 in England and Scotland, and a few thousand collectively in the other countries of Europe and in Australia. Small groups are also present in Hong Kong, Singapore, Sri Lanka, South Africa, and other Asian and African countries. Low birthrate, prohibition of the acceptance of converts, and a discouraging of intermarriage with members of other sectarian groups have contributed steadily to an overall, gradual, decline in demographic numbers. Women have come to play important leadership roles within the community during the past eighth to ten decades, including editing the most widely read newsletters in North America and South Asia wherein issues of significance to societal change are debated—on which see further chapter six.

The majority of Mazda-worshipers or Zoroastrians did not leave Iran, however. They stayed on, notwithstanding hardships of living as a confessional minority under a majority Muslim population after the thirteenth century C.E. (Choksy 1997). Surviving the asperities of time, their descendants continued the faith and its practices despite having to pay the poll tax to the Muslims for remaining Zoroastrian. Finally, in 1854 C.E., Parsis were able to send an emissary to the Qajar court in Iran to intercede on behalf of Iranian Zoroastrians and ensure that the poll tax was abolished (Boyce 1977). During the twentieth century C.E., a period of respite from economic hardship and the pressure of conversion to Islam was experienced under the two shahs (kings) of the anachronistically-named Pahlavi dynasty (1925–1979 C.E.) who promoted Zoroastrians to positions of authority, encouraged the expression of Mazdean socioreligious practices, and glorified Iran's ancient or pre-Islamic past. In 1966 C.E., there were nearly 60,000 Zoroastrians in Iran. However, the population there plummeted during the middle of the 1980s, after the Islamic revolution. Despite inflated figures in a 1988 census which put the community's membership at around 90,000, the number of Iranian Zoroastrians continues to decline as reflected by official revision downward of the population statistics to around 31,600 by 2000 C.E. This decline is the result of several factors: conversion to Bahaism is one, increased attempts to enforce conversion to Islam is another, and war between Iran and Iraq forced many Zoroastrians to immigrate in order to escape military conscription by finding refuge in the United States, Canada, Europe, Pakistan, and India. Although officially recognized as a minority and represented in national settings, Zoroastrians in Iran often are offered only limited protection from their Muslim neighbors by the Islamic regime that now governs the country. Nonetheless, Zoroastrians continue to survive not only in the central Iranian city of Yazd which has been their stronghold during recent centuries, but also at Tehran, Shiraz, Isfahan, and Khorramshahr, among other urban and rural locales. The religion's doctrines are taught to the male and female children, basic rites are still performed, visits to shrines (*pir*) retain popularity, and clerical and lay organizations remain active within the community. However, in Iran too, many socioreligious changes have occurred during the twentieth century C.E. under the influence both of the Parsis of India and of extensive contact with western societies (Boyce 1979:

218–223). These changes have significant impact on gender-relations, as will be analyzed in the sixth chapter of this book.

As discussed, when Zoroastrianism or Mazdaism gradually developed into a religion, it came to be based on cosmic and ethical dualism between order and disorder, righteousness and falsehood, good and evil, and this dualism was personified in a pair of primal spirits: Ahura Mazda and Angra Mainyu. According to Zoroastrian doctrine of late antiquity and the Middle Ages, Ahura Mazda, the righteous creator, became by definition a perfect, good, rational, and omniscient being from whom no evil can proceed, because the medieval magi believed that a perfect spirit could not produce imperfection (Shkand Gumanig Wizar 8: 101–110; compare Choksy 1989a: 2–4). For this reason, Zoroastrian theology expounded that Ahura Mazda created the spiritual and material worlds in light, completely pure and sinless. Hence, in the Zoroastrian ethos, disorder, darkness, sin, irreligiosity, deceit, strife, lust, decay, pollution, and death came to be perceived as aspects of evil, all shaped by the destructive spirit or Angra Mainyu (Videvdad 1: 1–20). By clearly separating the locus of evil from that of good, Zoroastrian diabology of late antiquity and the Middle Ages played a fundamental role in the history of religions, for Angra Mainyu represented the first clearly defined example of the devil as the principle of absolute evil (J. B. Russell 1988: 99).

Canonical Zoroastrianism identified both Ahura Mazda and Angra Mainyu as clearly masculine beings. Essentially, a male-dominated society ensured that, in Zoroastrianism, the origins of good and evil were attributed to male entities. To identify either or both the primal creator and the eternal nemesis as feminine would have been, within such a worldview, tantamount to yielding overwhelming authority and power over religion and society to women. Male perceptions barred the feminine from solely vesting either of the two opposite principles—good and evil (compare J. B. Russell 1988: 62). Needless to say, Zoroastrianism, like other major religious traditions, also presents no ambiguity regarding the gender of its male founder. It appears that the dynamics of control and power in patriarchal societies did not permit major religious leaders to be women.[5]

Humans, it was written by medieval magi, were produced by Ahura Mazda as his allies in the cosmic conflict according to the faith's theology (Bundahishn 3: 23-24; see further Choksy 1989a: 4-5). Zoroastrianism holds that the immortal spirit (*fravashi*, *frawahr*) of each human consented to assume corporeal form to battle Angra Mainyu. As a result of this covenant, each person's—whether male or female—religious function is to aid orderly righteousness by combating the chaotic forces of evil through every action performed during his or her lifetime. Good actions and adherence to divine law by people in the corporeal state are regarded as vital for the cosmic triumph of righteousness over evil on the spiritual level. The rewards of heaven, after death, are offered to the souls of believers who uphold good and counter evil during their lifetimes. The trials of hell await those who follow the evil espoused by Angra Mainyu (Choksy 1989a: 5-6). Disorder and falsehood, Zoroastrian equivalents of sin, result, at least in part, from violation of this personal bond with god (compare in general Ricoeur 1969: 50-54). Angra Mainyu and his negative spiritual legions are thought to be constantly active in the world, supposedly working through human form to corrupt the pure creations and lead them into disorder (see Shaked 1967: 227-228, 230-234).[6]

The Mazdean system of dualism, with its independent locus of evil and a combat theodicy in which humans supposedly are lured into violating rules of society regarded as sanctified by religious law, permitted human excesses, desires, and fears to be perceived as perpetuating evil, sin, and disorder on a cosmic scale. These views, of course, have some counterparts in the Judeo-Christian tradition (Forsyth 1989: 212-213, 216). Such a system functioned as a viable means for priests to attribute some blame to women, and thus away from men, and to caution that the feminine may further the cause of evil. Masculine and feminine have been viewed, at different times by members of many societies, as opposites in a strife-torn universe (Buchanan 1987: 434; J. B. Russell 1988: 60-62; Scott 1988: 43). Mazdean men, through their endeavor to uphold Ahura Mazda's will by the establishment of order represented by society and religious hierarchy, came to be depicted as the warriors of god—constantly having to counter the onslaught of the forces of the devil. Women, when in opposition to men, were construed as allies of Angra Mainyu and, hence, ignoble. By extension, as will be seen, the female became partially dangerous for Zoroastrians—allegedly at times a propagator of disorder, misery, lust, torment, and evil—despite their other positive religious and social roles.[7]

CHAPTER THREE

Deceit, Discord, Sexuality, & Avidity

The prime agent of the disorder, evil, or wickedness, allegedly embodied by Angra Mainyu in canonical Mazdaism or Zoroastrianism, was Drug (Druj) or Druz (Dro), "disorder, chaos," eventually equated to "lie, falsehood, unrighteousness" as mentioned in the previous chapter. Drug was regarded as the locus of all deceit (compare Gray 1929: 191–195; Zaehner 1961: 34–37; Kellens 1996b). A passage in the Gathas, incorporated into the Yasna liturgy of the Avesta, proclaims: "Of these two spirits, he who was of the lie [Drug] chose to do the worst things" (Yasna 30: 5). Indeed, Zarathushtra perceived Drug as the eternal adversary of Asha, "order, truth, righteousness," represented by Ahura Mazda (Yasna 31: 1, 51: 10; Yasht 10: 86). The Yashts and the Videvdad depict Drug united with Angra Mainyu and in direct opposition to Ahura Mazda: "We worship Sraosha, who is the most beneficent spirit's [Ahura Mazda's] watcher over Drug, who has not slept since the two spirits—both the beneficent spirit and the evil one—produced [their] creations," and "Zarathushtra asked Ahura Mazda, 'How shall I free the world from that Drug, from that evil-doer Angra Mainyu?'" (Yasna 57: 17; Yasht 11: 14; Videvdad 19: 12; Pahlavi Yasn or exegesis on the Yasna 30: 10). A ninth-century C.E. Pahlavi source claims even Ahura Mazda regards Angra Mainyu as analogous to Drug and on one occasion addressed the evil spirit saying: "You cannot do everything, O Drug!" (Wizidagiha i Zadspram, "Selections of Zadspram," 1: 6). As the foe of Asha and Ahura Mazda, Drug supposedly desires to wreck "the righteous material world" through deluded humans who "continue to destroy the creatures of truth due to the commandments of the lie" (Yasht 3: 17; Videvdad 8: 21; Yasna 31: 1). Further, the religion's demonology, as preserved in the Avesta, claims that the "house of the lie" is synonymous with hell, and is located toward the north—believed to be a diabolic region due to its association with cold and darkness (Yasna 46: 11, 49: 11, 51: 14; Yasht 3: 17; Videvdad 8: 21).

The religion's confession of faith or Fravarane, composed in late or Young Avestan dialect, enjoins devotees to "forsake the company of all this [evil] as belonging to Drug, as [being] contemptuous" (4: 2).[1] Another, much later, admonition to forswear the lie is preserved in the Wizidagiha i Zadspram where the advice was attributed to Zarathushtra: "Sever Drug from [your] mind" (27: 13). Every irreligious individual came to be denounced as a dregvant or drvant, "adherent to the lie" (Yasna 30: 4, 32: 5, 14, 46: 5, 48: 2, 51: 9). The contest between truth and lie, order and disorder, on material and spiritual levels became so central to Mazdaism that Zarathushtra depicted himself as devotional poet, in the Gathas, pleading of Ahura Mazda: "How might I deliver the lie [or disorder] into the hands of truth [or order] so as to vanquish it in accordance with your precepts" (Yasna 44: 14). He supposedly was instructed: "One can vanquish the lie with truth" (Yasna 48: 1; compare Yasna 49: 3). Rock inscriptions in the Old Persian language, commissioned by the Achaemenian monarch Darius or Darayavahush I (ruled 522–486 B.C.E.), reveal that rebellion—thought to cause social chaos—against the king of kings was attributed to the handiwork of the lie: "It was the lie [Drauga] who made them rebellious" (Behistun or Bisitun inscription 4: 34).[2] Consequently, Darius beseeched Ahura Mazda to "protect this land from the lie" (Persepolis inscription d: 18–20).

The terminology of the Avesta indicates that Zarathushtra and the early Mazdean community perceived Drug as feminine, although the Old Persian inscriptions indicate that the ancient Persians employed masculine grammatical gender when referring to this evil spirit (Bartholomae 1979: 778–781; Kent 1982: 192). By the time medieval exegeses and commentaries, the Zand and the Pahlavi books, were codified between the fourth and the twelfth centuries C.E., Drug had been transformed into a feminine personification of evil (compare Christensen 1941: 5). As a leader of demonic hosts she became an important representation of radical evil, for it was believed that "the harmfulness of Angra Mainyu is manifest through lying speech" (Bundahishn 1: 49). Much unhappiness was ascribed to this demoness (Zaehner 1961: 277). Her power to influence the wills, thoughts, words, and deeds of Zoroastrians, thus leading them astray into discord and chaos, was feared (Wiziriha i Den i Weh i Mazdesnan 6). She was believed to have caused the downfall of legendary figures, including Yima or Jam, the Iranian counterpart of the Indo-European first human named Yemo (compare Humbach 1996: 73–74). It was this representative of the demonic feminine that the immortal souls of humanity are said to have agreed to combat in their covenant with Ahura Mazda described in the Bundahishn, which dates from the ninth through the twelfth centuries C.E.: "incarnate you will battle the lie and vanquish it" (3: 23). She is condemned, daily, by the faithful in the Kem Na Mazda, a medieval prayer based on extracts from the Avesta: "Perish, O lie! Crawl away, O lie! Disappear, O lie! In the north you shall perish" (compare Vaetha Nask 70).[3] Epithets from that period describe the demoness as chaotic, life-destroying, consisting of darkness, and possessing a hideous countenance (Gray 1929: 192–193). Only at the end of time, after the twelve-thousand-year struggle between good and evil, will Drug be vanquished by Ahura Mazda, Asha, other deities, and men acting in unison (Yasna 30: 8, 48: 1; Yasht 19: 12; Denkard 332: 10–19).[4] The name of this demoness in its Pahlavi or Middle Persian form, Druz or Dro, even came to represent evil beings generally.

While Drug increasingly was regarded as the feminine manifestation of deceit, discord, and many other aspects thought to be evil, Asha or Ard remained constant in the literature as neuter—the righteous, orderly, principle that opposes female unrighteousness and disorder. The Iranian Asha, a complement of the Vedic Rta, is invoked on numerous occasions in the religious texts in antipathy to Drug (Boyce 1989: 200–201, 212). Pious male believers were regarded as ashavan, "follower(s) of order, adherent(s) to truth" (Yasna 34: 10; Yasht 10: 45). The rightly-ordered universe, excluding all chaotic evil within it, was extolled as the "world of Asha" (Yasna 31: 1). Only in premodern and modern times did Drug gain gender neutrality in popular parlance.

As mentioned previously, it was believed that the female Drug does not act alone. The Avesta recorded that she works evil in conjunction with two other female demonic spirits: Daiwi or Dawi, "Deceit," and Pairimaiti (Parimati) or Paromad, "Denial," who characterize apostasy and atheism respectively (Videvdad 19: 43; Yasna 32: 3).[5] By the seventh century C.E., Daiwi and Pairimaiti, in connection with the lie and the denial of truth, came to be identified as sources of disbelief in god and religion, a deception that was thought to result in men abandoning Mazda-worship, abstaining from religious belief, or else choosing to worship evil—all of which were held to result in disorder on the universal scale (compare Nerangestan II, 25a: 19, III, 9: 2). Pairimaiti, in turn, was said to deceive men in concord with another female demon named Taromaiti (Taromati) or Taromad, "Contempt, Scorn," also fashioned by Angra Mainyu (Yasht 3: 8, 11, 15). Innocuous at first, Taromaiti's depiction evolved over the following centuries into yet one more aspect of the demonic feminine. She came to symbolize evil which admits the existence of religion but denies the value of faith (Nerangestan II, 1: 1–3; compare Bundahishn 1: 55)—i.e., a spirit who realizes the need for order but chooses disorder. She supposedly beguiles men into espousing the lie and propagating heresy or irreligion rather than accepting the truth and spreading righteousness or religion (see further Gray 1929: 215). As such, this female demon—both feminine in grammatical gender and anthropomorphic descriptions—came to represent direct confrontation, through disobedience, with the social system sanctioned by Zoroastrianism (Bundahishn 27: 14). The authors of the Denkard went as far as to note "the evil spirit's [Angra Mainyu's] visible manifestation, through [presence of] the evil mind in the [human] will, can be discerned by thoughts of Taromaiti" (50: 9–10). The text adds that when united with the sensations "irreligion is intensified by Taromaiti and Pairimaiti" (Denkard 50: 17–19).

Taromaiti was portrayed by theologians between the fourth and the ninth centuries C.E. as being in opposition to the beneficent immortal Spenta Armaiti, the earth divinity and allegorical mother of humanity, on a spiritual level (Bundahishn 5: 1; Wiziriha i Den i Weh i Mazdesnan 6). The religious opposition between Taromaiti and Spenta Armaiti, contempt and devotion, mirrors the social tensions perceived in women by medieval Zoroastrian men—i.e., masculine views of the feminine. Spenta Armaiti was thought to make men holy, lead sinners back to grace, serve as the spiritual mother of people, and, as feminine earth divinity, ensure order, concord, and productivity (Yasna 31: 12, 48: 5; Videvdad 2: 10, 18, 3: 35; Bundahishn 3: 17; compare Bailey 1967: 139–142; Boyce 1987). As a model, unlike Taromaiti, she represents the pious, devoted female who will serve god and man as wife and mother working to ensure that cosmic order is upheld (compare Alishan 1989: 79–80). Yet, Spenta Armaiti was ranked only after the three masculine or neuter Amesha Spentas within the internal hierarchy assigned by the faith to those spirits (Windfuhr 1976: 273–286). Passive, she posed no danger to patriarchy. Taromaiti, on the other hand, together with the female demons Drug and Pairimaiti, presented aspects of the dangerous feminine—an allegorical image of deceit, contemptuousness, disobedience, and active rebellion against masculine domination. Women who chose to act like Taromaiti were tacitly condemned, for according to a notion preserved in the writings of a sixth-century C.E. cleric only a "virtuous woman of good character is the better assistant of peace" (Menog i Xrad, "[Book of] the Spirit of Wisdom," 14: 12). This notion of feminine disorder in Mazdaism has close parallels with, and perhaps influenced, the Islamic notion of *fitna*, "calamity, discord, disorder," which by the ninth century C.E. became synonymous with women (see Gardet 1964: 930–931; Spellberg 1988: 112–113). According to a religious tradition (*hadith*), preserved in the canonical collection of al-Tirmidhi (d. 892 C.E.), the prophet Muhammad is supposed to have said: "When a woman approaches you, she does so in the shape of a demonic spirit" (2: 413).

Zoroastrian demonology, however, is far more specific in its association of gender with evil as discord and disharmony than many other Near Eastern and South Asian religions. The demonic feminine is essentially disruption and destruction closely linked to a notion of ambiguity, secrecy, and deceit in woman's ascribed powers (generally compare Auerbach 1982: 1–2, 8). Evil women were decried as a perpetrator of evil on men who thus could view themselves as beguiled victims. For example, in Mazdaism, disobedience was represented by the demoness Asrushti, who acts with the archdemon Aka

Manah or Akoman, "Evil Mind," to ferment strife and turmoil (Yasna 33: 4). Zarathushtra, in the Gathas, lamented that individuals who have been deceived by Asrushti "do not turn [their] attention toward the care and companionship of truth, nor delight in the counsel of good thoughts" (Yasna 44: 13). Strife itself was symbolized in the Avesta by yet another female demonic entity, Anaxshti (Yasna 60: 5). Male dominance over the female in maintaining socioreligious order came to be reflected in this ancient diabology, for the devotional literature claimed that feminine disobedience and strife, Asrushti and Anaxshti respectively, would eventually be overcome by masculine obedience and steadfastness of duty in the form of the male spiritual beings Sraosha and Mithra (Yasna 60: 5; Yasht 10: 29).[6]

Another female demon, Bushyasta or Bushasp, "Sloth, Procrastination," allegedly assists Angra Mainyu, Drug, and other demonesses in endeavors to lead men astray into chaos it was believed (Yasht 18: 2; Videvdad 11: 9, 18: 16, 24; see also Gray 1929: 202–203; Williams 1990a). The faith's early and medieval writings claim that she lulls men into laziness, slumber, and neglect of religious duty, thereby permitting cosmic order to disintegrate (Videvdad 18: 16; Bundahishn 27: 32). Sloth presented a particularly baneful malediction to medieval Zoroastrian clerics (Dadestan i Denig 36: 31, 39), for indifference by devotees often led to a decline in temple offerings, failure to adhere to religious law, and lack of deference to the ruling hierarchy of kings and priests. For example, the Tosar nama, "Letter of Tosar [or Tansar]"—a third-century C.E. document, revised in the sixth century C.E., then translated into Arabic and later New Persian—recorded that neglect of the faith supposedly led to a situation where "corruption became widespread; men ceased to submit to religion, reason, and the state; [and] all sense of value vanished" in the period just preceding the Sasanian dynasty (14). This female demon's far-reaching power was epitomized in the epithet "long-handed" for she was even thought to strike at birth (Yasht 10: 97, 134; Videvdad 11: 9; Denkard 356: 6–8).

The apathy that Bushyasta casts upon individuals could hypothetically be driven away not by devotees but by the mighty male spiritual being Mithra, divinity of the contract—specifically the primeval covenant between Ahura Mazda and the immortal souls of men—

who enforces duty, service, and worship (Yasht 10: 97, 134). Mithra was said to be aided in this task by the feminine mirror image of sloth, the female divinity Arshtat or Ashtad, "Rectitude, Justice," who ensures that men fulfill their proper duties (Yasht 18: 2; see also Gnoli 1987). Hence, from the standpoint of a male-oriented religion, a feminine vice is counteracted and the prevalent social order reinforced by a representative of the masculine gender whose assistant is an appropriately servile female spirit. Another divinity, Manthra Spenta or Maraspand, "Holy Word," was also believed to be involved in attempts to rein in Bushyasta (Wiziriha i Den i Weh i Mazdesnan 7). By the late medieval period, however, a process of de-demonization had begun, one which transformed the Pahlavi Bushasp into an amorphous, yet still dangerous, creature who casts sleep, dreams, and delusion upon humans (Asmussen 1982: 117–119). This change may indicate that the rigid demonology characteristic of the Sasanian ecclesiastic hierarchy declined after the Arab Muslim conquest of Zoroastrian Iran reduced the magi's influence.

The dualism of good and evil is also reflected in the schism between religion and sexuality (Savramis 1974: viii; Elliott 1999: 2, 6). In the Mazdean case it was the cause of a morality which, unlike Christianity but like the Hindu tradition, did not reject much that was sexual, yet viewed sexual profligacy as a prime example of human excess, disorderly conduct, and feminine evil (compare in general Savramis 1974: 4–5, 52–57, 68; O'Flaherty 1980: 27–29; Brown 1988: 19–20). Sexuality, while not completely equated with chaos and evil, came to be regarded as socially disruptive and a cause of individual harm. Associated with demonology, feminine sexuality provided a religiously-sanctioned solution to the theological implication of male sexual desire possibly being connected with evil. Blame was shifted disproportionately to the feminine which then came to be condemned as the instigator of masculine desire and sexual excess in many faiths (compare Brown 1988: 33–64, 93–102; Forsyth 1989: 212–213, 216). Yet, sex and sexuality are essential in Zoroastrianism, for the begetting of children brings individuals into the material world to do battle against the evil spirit (Choksy 1989a: 88–89). Consequently, Zoroastrianism, like Judaism, sought to neutralize those aspects of the feminine—the alluring and the desirable—which men found dangerous, while promoting the procreative function as essential (Bird 1974: 58–59; Savramis 1974: 68; Brown 1988: 85–86; Forsyth 1989: 155–156, 181).

The ambiguity in Mazdean attitudes toward feminine sexuality, transferred from theology to society and resulting in a view of woman as an admixture of good and evil, was reflected in the Bundahishn. Therein, it was claimed that Ahura Mazda had admonished women:

> I created you, whose adversary is the class of whores. You were created with an orifice close to your buttocks, and sexual intercourse seems to you like the taste of the sweetest food is to the mouth. You are my helper for man is born from you. Yet, you cause me, Ahura Mazda, grief. If I had found another vessel from which to produce man, I would never have created you. I searched the water, earth, plants, beneficial animals, on the highest mountains, and in the deepest rivers, but did not find a vessel from which the righteous man could be [created] except woman. (14a: 1)

Here, the link between sex, food, woman, and evil was presented through the words of the god Ahura Mazda (see further Choksy 1988a: 75–76, 79).

Male fear of female sexuality came to be captured in the personas attributed to four demonesses. Foremost is Jahika (Jahi) or Jeh, "Whore," allegedly the fiend of lust and debauchery. She is mentioned only fleetingly in the Avesta (Yasna 9: 32; Yasht 3: 9, 12, 16; Videvdad 18: 62, 21: 1, 17). Yet, with the reinforcement of negative views under the influence of dualism during the Middle Ages, Jahika quickly came to be portrayed as a mistress and handmaiden of Angra Mainyu (Gray 1929: 206; Zaehner 1961: 231–235; 1972: 183–195; Choksy 1988a: 77–79; 1989a: 95–96; compare J. B. Russell 1988: 117). Medieval Zoroastrian cosmogony portrayed her as the devil's strong ally from the very inception of the universal antagonism. According to the myth of creation, she even revitalized Angra Mainyu after Ahura Mazda and man had scored an initial success:

> When the evil spirit saw that he, himself, and all the other demonic spirits were fully powerless on account of the righteous man, he [Angra Mainyu] was stupefied. He lay in a stupor for three thou-

sand years. While he was stupefied, the chief demons cackled one by one, "Arise, our father, for we will wage war in the material world [so] that Ahura Mazda and the beneficent immortals [will suffer] distress and harm." One by one, they related their own [future] evil deeds in detail. But the accused evil spirit was not comforted by this and did not arise from that stupor for fear of the righteous man, until the accursed Whore demoness came [forth] after three thousand years. She cackled, "Arise, our father, for in that battle I will cast so much affliction upon the righteous man and the toiling bull that, owing to my deeds, they will not be fit to live. I will steal their glory. I will harm the water, earth, fire, and plants. I will harm all the creations that Ahura Mazda created." She related those [future] evil deeds in such great detail that Angra Mainyu was comforted finally, arose from that stupor, and kissed the Whore's face. (Bundahishn 4: 1–5)

Thus, this feminine demonic spirit was believed to have aided in vanquishing Gayo-Maretan, the primeval androgyne, at the beginning of evil's invasion into the material world, and continues—in religious thought—to entice men both directly and through her mortal female counterparts. Once again, the Bundahishn recorded this myth: "[When Angra Mainyu had arisen from his stupor] he exclaimed to the Whore demoness, 'Ask for whatever you desire so that I may grant it to you.' Ahura Mazda in his omniscience knew at that moment the evil spirit would grant whatever the Whore demoness desired and that there could be great advantage to him. A being in the form of a fifteen-year-old youth was revealed to the Whore demoness who fastened her thoughts on him. The Whore demoness cried out to the evil spirit, 'Give me lust for man so that I may seat him in the house as my lord'" (4: 6–8). As the archetype for the notion of woman as seductress and unworthy companion, Jahika came to be regarded as the patroness of evil women—the adversary of chaste women, faithful wives, and trustworthy female companions (see further Zaehner 1972: 187–188; 1976: 44). Indeed, another passage in the Bundahishn claims that "the Whore [demoness] opposes [righteous] women" (5: 3). Zadspram, reflecting medieval theology, expounded in his Wizidagiha: "When Angra Mainyu scuttled into creation, he had the irreligious brood of the Whore demoness as his companions, just as a man [should] have women of good stature. For indeed, the Whore is a demon. He [Angra Mainyu] appointed the Whore demoness leader of her brood, the leader of all whores, the most grievous adversary of the righteous man. He [Angra Mainyu] coupled himself to the irreligious Whore demoness. He coupled himself to her for the corruption of women so that she [Jahika] might defile women, and the women because they were defiled may corrupt men and cause [men] to abandon their proper [religious] duties" (34: 30–31).[7]

Zoroastrian priests and theologians urged women not to succumb to Angra Mainyu's invasion of the body and not to follow Jahika's wanton ways. They also enjoined men to constantly struggle against lust.[8] The Pahlavi form of this demoness' name, Jeh, also denoted all harlots. As mentioned earlier, Jahika was regarded as the icon only of women who sought to beguile men, not of all women—for modest wives, mothers, sisters, and daughters were believed to aid men in the struggle against feminine evil. Adurbad the son of Maraspand, a highpriest under Sasanian rule in the fourth century C.E., was recorded as advising men "to cherish the woman who is modest and marry her" and "not to forsake the righteous law for lust" (Pahlavi Texts 62: 50, 54, 149: 45). Once again, the Muslim notion of *fitna* bears relevance. Pictured as a beautiful young woman, *fitna* presents the disruptive power of female sexuality—chaos which is provoked and initiated by the feminine (Mernissi 1987: 31, 41–42, 53–54).

Later on, Iranian Muslim lyric poets such as Daqiqi (d. 978 C.E.) who composed in New Persian depicted the female form as seen through the beguiling silky veil of ardor—the blackness of dark hair, the brightness of rosy cheeks, the well-polished agate of lips (compare Moayyad 1988: 124–125). The heroic and romantic epics, two other genres of New Persian literature, also reflected this image of woman—best seen in the Shah nama, "Book of Kings," composed by Abu 'l-Qasem Ferdowsi (ca. 940–1020 C.E.) who drew upon earlier traditions when depicting women like Rudaba, Sudaba, Golnar, and Gordiya. The romantic epic Vis o Ramin, composed in the eleventh century C.E. but based on Parthian legends, portrayed Vis as "a spring garden where bright tulips grow. Its violets are her curls, its narcissus are her eyes. Her black curls are ripe grapes, her chin is an apple, her breasts are twin pomegranates. [Her body is] a royal treasury containing the heart's desire of all the world, her cheeks are brocade, her limbs are silk, her body is silver, her lips are bright rubies, her teeth are lustrous pearls" (26). Even descriptions of female wine stewards, usually regarded as Zoroastrian because magi owned many of the taverns, highlighted the aspect of sensuality (Grabar and others 1967: 35–36). Such imagery clearly hearkens back to Avestan and Middle Persian precursors such as the Yasht dedicated to Ashi (Ard, also Ahrishwang), the female divinity of fortune and recompense, in which virtuous young women—like the divine being they supposedly should mirror—were described as "narrow-waisted, fair-bodied, long-fingered, [so] beautiful in form as to delight beholders" (17: 11). Ashi was an Old Avestan abstract notion that came to be both divinized and personified in the literature of the Young Avesta and the Pahlavi books (Schlerath 1985a: 674; Kellens 2000: 7). Another text, Xusro ud Redag, "Xusro and the Page," a Pahlavi didactic work of prose set in the reign of Xusro I (ruled 531–579 C.E.), had described the ideal woman as one whose "head, buttocks, and neck are shapely, feet are small, waist is slender, breasts are like quinces, eyes are like almonds, [and] locks are black, lustrous, and long" (96).

Coupled with the New Persian images of woman, food, and precious objects is also preserved the notion of feminine sensuality as potentially dangerous to established human and divine order and, hence, evil. Woman reflected "scorpion curls" and the "sting of the scorpion" for Daqiqi (Moayyad 1988: 125). In Vis o Ramin, the poet placed a denouncement of female sexuality in the words of the heroine herself: "Women have more desire than shame and propriety. Women are created incomplete. Thus, they are self-obsessed and of ill-repute" (90). The Qabus nama, an eleventh-century C.E. mirror for princes or guidance manual, also referred to the presumed coquettish nature of women and their alleged excessive need for sexual gratification (71, 119). Like the medieval Zoroastrian authors of the Pahlavi Texts, its writer too urged men only to marry women who are "chaste, of sound faith, [and] modest" (117).

Next in the tetrad of female demons associated with sexuality is

Azi or Az, "Concupiscence," supposedly a diabolic manifestation of lust and avarice (Gray 1929: 202; Asmussen 1989: 168–169). Azi played only a minor role in the Avesta, extinguishing fires, and was countered by the divinity Xvarenah or Xwarrah (Farr), "Glory," supposedly working in unison with the sacrificial fat and milk offerings of men (Yasna 16: 8; Yasht 18: 1; Videvdad 18: 19, 21–22). The Avestan Azi has been often regarded by scholars as male for this spirit bears a masculine epithet *Daevo-data*, "demon-spawned" (Bartholomae 1979: 343, 671–672). Yet, it is probable that the epithet's grammatical gender is misleading, and early Zoroastrians thought of Azi as a demoness.[9] Az as depicted in the Zoroastrian Pahlavi books must be considered a female entity, despite Middle Persian lacking grammatical gender, based on contexts in which this spirit is spoken of as a feminine companion of Angra Mainyu. Furthermore, the medieval Zoroastrian demoness was gradually transformed into the mythological feminine symbol of immoderation under the influence of Manichaeism, a faith in which Az was clearly female for she is called "the wicked mother of all the demonic spirits" (S 9; Boyce 1975: 100).[10]

Medieval Mazdaism, like Manichaeism, portrayed this female demonic being as a prime mover in the evil spirit's attempts to ensnare the human soul in a debased corporeality and thus prevent its salvation—thereby disrupting the orderly progression of cosmic events (compare BeDuhn 2000: 104–105). Zadspram's Wizidagiha, reflecting influence of the Zurvanite sect and of Manichaeism, preserves vivid details of Azi as a mistress of demonic legions: "He [Angra Mainyu] chose as general of the commanders [of evil] none other than Azi. He assigned four lieutenants to assist her—namely wrath, winter, decrepitude, and woe—as [the heads of] the east, west, south, and north. Azi chose [as] leaders, the heads of the right and left, namely hunger and thirst. Likewise, decrepitude chose lamentation and mourning, and woe chose excess and deficiency" (34: 32–33; compare M 7984; Boyce 1975: 72). She was thought to encompass all evil and her food was said to be the creatures of Ahura Mazda (Wizidagiha i Zadspram 34: 35, 38). It came to be believed that, through avarice, she produces situations in which men are deprived of food and drink and eventually succumb to death

(Denkard 316: 9–17). Her perceived role as a feminine personification of evil came to be reinforced through association with the downfall of the primeval androgyne Gayo-Maretan and of men who indulge their desires (Bundahishn 4: 19).

In essence, this female demon appears to incorporate male fears surrounding the havoc created by social excesses involving sex, greed, and lack of control. One Middle Persian text noted that she "will not be sated, even if the entire world yielded to her" and her "covetous eye is an abode that is limitless" (Bundahishn 27: 33–34). Other sources depicted her as "most malcontent and most rapacious" and "the most oppressive of demonic spirits" (Pahlavi Texts 89: 32; Denkard 569: 14). As the opponent of contentment and moderation—sexual and corporeal—Azi became a tool by which society's strife and woes were demonized and attributed to the feminine, the female, and women. Darkness and disorder had, for medieval Zoroastrians and Manichaeans, a hunger that was insatiable, an evil craving thought to be partially embodied by the feminine (Denkard 836: 11; Xwastwanift I B; Asmussen 1965: 193; BeDuhn 2000: 50).

Azi was also regarded by Zoroastrians as so powerful, through the nexus of sexuality with avidity, that it came to be alleged she would remain a problem for men and their social order until the final apocalypse. Even at the end of time, she supposedly would attempt to resist the attempts of divine beings and men to impose universal order (Bundahishn 34: 28; Wizidagiha i Zadspram 34: 42–43). Unable to devour men any more, according to Zoroastrian eschatology of the tenth century C.E., she would then proceed to consume her former allies: "First she will devour wrath of the bloody spear, second the demon-created winter, third woe who moves in secret, and fourth decrepitude whose breath is foul, so none remain except Angra Mainyu and Azi. [Then] Azi the demon-spawned will cackle to Angra Mainyu 'I will devour you, O one of evil knowledge, for the divinities have taken away [all the other] creatures" (Pahlavi Rivayat Accompanying the Dadestan i Denig 48: 91–92). Trapped by Ahura Mazda, other divine spirits, and men, and facing annihilation at the hands of Azi, the devil supposedly will choose to capitulate to the masculine forces of good and be eternally banished from the universe rather than be consumed by the diabolical feminine. Azi, herself, then will be vanquished forever by the male good spirits Sraosha, Mithra, and Verethraghna or Wahram, the male divinity of victory (Bundahishn 34: 28–30; Wizidagiha i Zadspram 34: 44–45; Pahlavi Rivayat Accompanying the Dadestan i Denig 48: 93–96; Wiziriha i Den i Weh i Mazdesnan 7; see further Sundermann 1978: 494, 497–498). So, once again, in eschatology as in daily life, the religion presented eventual male dominance over the female, the divine masculine over the demonic feminine, good over evil, harmony over disharmony, order over disorder.

Two other female demons associated with the disruption attributed to sexuality and avidity were Xnathaiti, "Prurience, Lewdness," and Uta or Udag, "Loquacity" (Justi 1895: 332–333; Jackson 1928: 92–93; Gray 1929: 215, 218). Xnathaiti was first mentioned in the Avestan Videvdad as a creature of Angra Mainyu in conflict with Zarathushtra and the religion of Ahura Mazda (19: 5). Uta initially appeared in the Pahlavi exegesis on the Videvdad as the female demoness responsible for chatter and uncontrolled speech (Pahlavi Wendidad 18: 30). Conceited speech and violation of religiously-ordained periods of silence, as when dining and performing ritual ablutions and body functions, were attributed to this demoness in medieval times (Bundahishn 27: 23). Uta was equated with lust because of a myth that she was the first adulteress, whose sexual license disrupted human lineage and the transmission of social authority. She also was regarded as the mother of the mythic tyrant Azhi Dahaka or Azdahag and of other evil progeny (Dadestan i Denig 71: 5). During the sixth century C.E., Zoroastrian commentators denounced Uta as the "evil one" who all righteous men should spurn because of her disruptive power (Menog i Xrad 57: 25; compare Gray 1929: 215). Xnathaiti's evil domain, on the other hand, was extended beyond sexuality to encompass idolatry, probably because uncontrolled desire, like idol worship, was regarded as a consequence of irreligious behavior (Pahlavi Wendidad 19: 5).

At the opposite pole of this male-constructed notion of sexuality are found the female deities Spenta Armaiti (mentioned previously as an opponent of the demoness Taromaiti), Aredwi Sura Anahita, Ashi (mentioned previously in reference to feminine beauty), and Drvaspa. Armaiti initially represented the abstract notion of correct disposition during rituals (compare Kellens 2000: 8, 18, 48). As Spenta Armaiti, by medieval times her image developed into the personified divine companion of Ahura Mazda and the mother of creation. Thus, she became the spiritual symbol of chaste love—a celestial manifestation of perfect, ordered, existence praised by devotional poet, priests, and lay devotees alike. The composite, medieval, image of this spirit, captured in the Pahlavi Rivayat Accompanying the Dadestan i Denig, projected a domestic serenity that fit perfectly with dualism:

> It is revealed that when Zarathushtra sat in front of Ahura Mazda, and Vohu Manah, Asha Vahishta, Xshathra Vairya, Haurvatat, Ameretat, and Spenta Armaiti were seated close, Spenta Armaiti sat in his [Ahura Mazda's] embrace and her arm lay upon his neck. Zarathushtra asked Ahura Mazda, "Who is sitting in your embrace, who loves you so much and is so dear to you? You, Ahura Mazda, do not avert your gaze from her nor does she avert her gaze from you. You, Ahura Mazda, do not release her from your arms nor does she release you from her arms." Ahura Mazda replied, "This is Spenta Armaiti my daughter, my house-mistress of paradise, and the mother of creation." (8: 2–4)[11]

This literary image of Spenta Armaiti depicted aspects of female sexuality that the faith regarded as positive—submissiveness, devotion, and motherhood. While her demonic spiritual opponents seek to destroy men and the cosmos through lust, deceit, strife, and sloth, Spenta Armaiti ceaselessly cares for the earth, protects pious men and women, grants life, and remains forever loyal to Ahura Mazda in Zoroastrian theology (Boyce 1989: 204, 206–207, 313; Choksy 1989a: 10–11, 67, 121). In her role as earth spirit, she supposedly bears not only humanity but all useful animals and plants into the world to further divine will, religious law, and social order as established by god and man. Like her mortal counterparts, this divine spirit incorporates the "element of creation [and] production" (Denkard 415: 5–6). Chaste and obedient to male wishes, she eventually would be venerated as the "mother of religion" (Wizidagiha i Zadspram 4: 8).

Only a brief physical description of Spenta Armaiti is extant. The medieval passage in question links the female spirit to revelation and then highlights her role as a model for women to emulate:

> The religion was revealed by Spenta Armaiti at that time. She was the respondent [to] the non-Aryans at the house of Manushchihr, lord of the land of the Aryans, [in] the form of a woman. She appeared thus: She was wearing a luminous garment which shone forth in all directions. Around her waist was tied a golden sacred girdle which, itself, represented the religion of the Mazdeans. Thereafter, the other women who saw Spenta Armaiti [with] the sacred girdle were eager to tie sacred girdles [on themselves] so as to look beautiful. (Wizidagiha i Zadspram 4: 4–7)

This divinity's counterpart among the Sakas or Scythians of Central Asia was the Buddhist earth spirit S's'andramata whose anthropomorphic depiction was an attractive woman (Bailey 1967: 137–138, 142–143; Azarpay 1981: 138–139).

Aredwi Sura Anahita or Ardwisur Anahid is the Mazdean divinity of water, fertility, and authority. Her cult was widespread under the Achaemenians, Seleucids (312–175 B.C.E.), Parthians, and Sasanians—not only in Iran but even among Mazda-worshipers in Anatolia (see further Boyce 1982: 218–221; 1991: 46–47; Colledge 1986: 4, 8; Boyce and Grenet 1991: 202–205, 213–216, 224–235, 243–247, 264). The Achaemenian king of kings Artaxerxes or Artaxshassa II Mnemon (ruled 404–359 B.C.E.) gave thanks to her and also sought her protection, "may Ahura Mazda, Anahita, and Mithra protect me from all evil," in his Old Persian inscriptions (Susa a: 4–5; Susa d: 3–4; Hamadan a: 5–6). The Sasanian royal family's sacred fire, Adur Anahid, at the city of Istakhr burned in this feminine divinity's honor (Boyce 1979: 106, 114). By the Middle Ages, Anahita's attributes had come to include not only those of her Avestan namesake, but also those of the Mesopotamian deity Ishtar with whom she had been fused at an early date. She even assimilated attributes of Ashi an Iranian divinity of fortune, Harahvaiti-Sarasvati an Indo-Iranian river spirit, and Artemis the Greek divinity of chastity and hunting.[12] Indeed, the Young Avestan devotional poem (Yasht 5) dedicated to her had been modified by the time Zoroastrian scripture was codified and, thus, included allusions both to her ancient roles and to her medieval ones.

FIGURE 1. SASANIAN SILVER COIN IMAGES OF ANAHITA. Late third century C.E. *Courtesy of the American Numismatic Society, New York.*

Her name consists of three appellations "[the] Moist, Strong, [and] Undefiled [one]" (compare Yasht 1: 21, 5: 1; Visperad, "All of the Lords," 1: 5). She was said to protect and supervise worldly affairs, and to bestow victory and kingship upon leaders who uphold all the tenets of Zoroastrianism (Yasht 5: 23, 26, 46, 50, 89). Thus, Anahita came to be depicted on rock reliefs and coins (obverse and reverse of figure 1) of the Sasanian period as conferring the diadem of sovereignty upon monarchs (see further Choksy 1988b: 44–46; 1989b: 126–133). She was thought to grant wisdom to priests (Yasht 5: 86). She cleanses the earth and waters (Yasht 5: 5; Bundahishn 3: 17). She supposedly "purifies the semen of all men, purifies for conception the wombs of all women, grants easy childbirth to all women, [and] grants milk to all women regularly and at the proper time" (Yasht 5: 2; compare Yasht 5: 5, 87). She was thought to regulate every aspect of birth (Yasna 65: 1–2; Yasht 5: 2; Videvdad 7: 16). The devotional poem in her praise proclaims: "Maidens ready for marriage ask [you] for a noble lord and a strong master of the house. Young wives in labor ask [you] for easy childbirth. You, O Aredwi Sura Anahita, have the power to grant those [boons] to them" (Yasht 5: 87). Zoroastrian eschatology even recorded a belief that this female spiritual entity preserves Zarathushtra's semen in the mythical Lake Kayansih from whence the three saviors will arise during the final days of humanity (Bundahishn 33: 36). Again, overtones of socioreligious order are clear.

As already mentioned, feminine physical representations of

Aredwi Sura Anahita are found in the Zoroastrian visual arts (figure 1) at least from late antiquity, especially the Sasanian period. Images of her may have existed even earlier during Achaemenian and Parthian times when statutes are supposed to have been crafted as part of a temple cult (compare among others Boyce 1982: 203–204; Dandamayev and Lukonin 1989: 269–270). It appears that those visual depictions were modeled along a more ancient devotional narrative, an Avestan—probably pre-Zoroastrian—poem which was modified and included in Zoroastrian liturgy, that still is recited by devotees as part of her veneration:

> Aredwi Sura Anahita is always seen in the form of a beautiful woman, strong, well-formed, high-girded, statuesque, noble, of very high birth, dressed in a very precious pleated golden garment. Aredwi Sura Anahita, [who is] of noble birth, [when] displaying her rectangular golden earrings, always wears a necklace around her fine neck. She girds herself around the waist so that [her] breasts are well-shaped and prominent. Upon her head, Aredwi Sura Anahita wears a resplendent, well-crafted, golden diadem. [Upon her body, she] wears beaver-skin robes. (Yasht 5: 126–129)[13]

Anahita's noble lineage and qualities contrast with the base origins of Jahika and Uta. Her narrative attractiveness contrasts with the repulsiveness of Drug. Yet, despite the beauty attributed to her, this divinity's main characteristic is denoted by the epithet *anahita*, "undefiled," whereby she was referred to constantly. As a divinity she is untouched by men, as water she is clean of all impurity (compare Yast 5: 1). Among the Armenians, whose pre-Christian society was deeply influenced by Iranian culture and by Zoroastrianism, she served as the archetype of chastity (Alishan 1989: 82). Her chastity thus stands in stark contrast to the sexual license of Jahika, Azi, Xnathaiti, and Uta. It appears likely that Aredwi Sura Anahita's asexual nature had been established, with those attributes inherited from Ishtar which bore traces of sexual liberty suppressed, by the time codification of the Avesta took place. She even garnered male prowess, described in combat and chariot-racing scenes (Yasht 5: 11, 13). Hence, the image of chastity and semi-masculinity created for her by Zoroastrian priests would have served as a standard against which other medieval images of the feminine—divine, demonic, spiritual, and mortal—were compared and contrasted. As models for Zoroastrian women, the scriptural and artistic depictions of Anahita were ones to be emulated—to whatever extent possible, and within the limitations of human existence. From a social viewpoint, emulation of this divine spirit's attributes by mortal members of the feminine gender would have been encouraged within the parameters of chastity and support for pious men preached by the faith. But like Mary, the mother of Jesus Christ, who become an icon for Christian women, the Iranian divinity Anahita eventually denoted an unattainable ideal for Mazdean women.

Drvaspa or Druwasp, a feminine divinity of health, healing, and protection is mentioned in the Avesta (Yasht 9; Siroza, "Invocations for Thirty Days," I: 14, II: 14) and briefly in the Pahlavi sources (Supplementary Texts to the Shayest ne Shayest, "Proper and the Improper," 11: 4). Many of her attributes, like the ritual invocations of her, appear to be derived from those of Ashi—even though Drvaspa may have had counterparts in Vedic rites, attesting to her original veneration as an independent spiritual entity. After assimilation into Zoroastrianism, she was said to have been *Mazda-dhata*, "created by [Ahura] Mazda" (Bartholomae 1979: 783, 1159). Within established Zoroastrian praxis, she then came to be venerated for providing good health, healing, and protection derived from the wise lord. She was associated with horses, as her name denotes, and cattle. Like Anahita, Drvaspa was said to be strong and to serve as an upholder of order. Thus, her spiritual functions became those of a feminine entity who assists the masculine god Ahura Mazda (see further Gray 1929: 73–75; Boyce 1989: 82; Kellens 1996c: 565). In the iconography of the Kushan kingdom (ca. 41–226 C.E.), she appears to have undergone a transformation due to her association with horses, riding, and chariotry—giving up her femininity in that multivalent religious setting for the socially preferred masculine gender (Christensen 1928: 39; Göbl 1984: plates 7, 20, 165).

Deceit, discord, uncontrolled sexuality, and avidity, in contrast to veracity, concord, chastity, and restraint, were social phenomena which took on larger dimensions in Zoroastrianism within a dualistic religious universe that held order to be supreme (compare in part

Kloppenborg 1995: viii). Concerns for the well-being of the community of believers resulted in particular aspects of human behavior which were not regarded as beneficial coming to be given facets that linked those actions directly to evil. Such developments were not unique to the Zoroastrian faith. The emphasis placed by the medieval mowbeds and herbeds (the latter were religious officials, of lower rank than full-fledged magi because they did not officiate at central rites, who may have come to serve as clerical teachers and theologians) on defining those features as negative and then connecting them to the feminine gender also finds a counterpart among medieval Christianity (compare Elliott 1999: 37–38, 52–56). Despite such common themes, however, the specific manners in which the clerics made such connections between the negative features of religion and the feminine were uniquely Zoroastrian and were based on the faith's dualistic need to ensure cosmic order is maintained through appropriate actions. An absence of theology written by female members of the Zoroastrian community in ancient and medieval times results in the images projected by male clerics serving as the only reflections of how these issues were viewed. The absence of women's writings, notwithstanding, it is unlikely that members of both gender's perceived their religious constructs in identical manners. Thus, faith and devotion may very well have impinged upon their lives differentially.

CHAPTER FOUR

Weakness, Imperfection, & Death

The danger projected by men, male religion, and masculine society on female sexuality as potentially representing disorder came to be linked closely to a belief that women as individuals and the feminine as a gender often were weak willed, easily tempted, and led astray by the devil's horde. Whereas female demons are considered evil by nature, this was not regarded as the universal case for women. Rather, Mazdean dogma suggested that hasty action and failure to resist the wily ways of Angra Mainyu, the male demons, and the female demons lead women to fermenting chaos and producing sinful actions. This was, from the religious perspective, a major imperfection. Once again, the Bundahishn recorded a myth that disseminated and reinforced this notion by ascribing it to acts of the first woman Mashyana or Mahriyana. Mashyana, together with her male counterpart Mashya or Mahra, supposedly arose of a rhubarb plant that grew from the semen of the primeval androgyne Gayo-Maretan after it had been slain by Angra Mainyu, Jahika, and other evil spirits (Bundahishn 14: 1–10).[1] Hence unlike in Judeo-Christian belief, woman was not created from man—rather, a unity of human creation was believed to have occurred with both genders fully equal in all respects at the time of origin. Moreover, unlike in the Bible or the Qur'an, the creation story codified in the Bundahishn can by no means be construed as laying blame for disobedience to god on the first woman alone—for both Mashya and Mashyana sinned together initially. Yet the co-creation and joint-culpability of the first human couple does not imply continued equality of the genders over time, for the first unrighteous action was said to be compounded shortly thereafter by an irreligious ritual act on the part of Mashyana alone.

According to the major version of this myth as preserved after several renditions:

> Ahura Mazda said to Mashya and Mashyana, "You are mortal, the parents of the world. Perform your tasks in accordance with religious law and with pure mind. Think, speak, and do good. Do not worship the demons." ... The first words they spoke were "Ahura Mazda created water, earth, plants, animals, the stars, the moon, the sun, and all fruitful things." ... Then, the adversary [Angra Mainyu] beguiled their minds and corrupted them. So they exclaimed, "Angra Mainyu created water, earth, plants, and all other things." When they pronounced this first lie, which ruined them, they spoke in concordance with the will of the demons. For this lie, both of them [Mashya and Mashyana] were damned and their souls will remain in hell until the final resurrection. The demons became more malevolent, owing to the impiety they [Mashya and Mashyana] had displayed. Owing to their [evil deeds], they [Mashya and Mashyana] became wildly envious of each other. They attacked, struck, and wounded one other, and ripped each other's hair. Then the demonic spirits cried out from the gloom, "You are mortal; worship the demonic spirits so that your envy may subside." Mashyana sprang forth, milked a cow, and poured [its milk] toward the north [hell]. The demonic spirits were greatly invigorated by that act of evil-worship. (Bundahishn 14: 11–29)

The tale of the first mortal couple's fall from grace bears a moral which would not have been lost on Zoroastrian audiences: weakness of character results in irreligious deeds, and disruption of order that produces evil is a direct consequence of such actions. It was, like the biblical account of the Fall, meant to serve as a didactic, warning, tale (compare Auerbach 1982: 157). Broad parallels clearly exist between the tale of Mashya and Mashyana and the biblical legend of Adam, Eve, the serpent, and the Fall (Genesis 2: 4–3: 24).[2] More importantly, this primordial-twin myth probably evolved not during Zarathushtra's own time but after Iranians had political hegemony over the Near East between the sixth and the fourth centuries B.C.E. —even though evidence from a Bactrian-Margiana Archeological

·WEAKNESS, IMPERFECTION, DEATH·   53

FIGURE 2. TEMPTATION OF MASHYA AND MASHYANA. Illustration from an Athar al-baqiya manuscript by al-Biruni (d. ca. 1048 C.E.). Early fourteenth century C.E. *Courtesy of the Edinburgh University Library, Scotland (Or. Ms. 161, folio 48 verso)*.

Complex seal suggests that the Gayo-Maretan legend may be pre-Zoroastrian (see further Choksy forthcoming).

At that time, the original, mythic, Indo-Iranian primeval twins Yima or Jam and Yimi or Jamag, counterparts of the Vedic Yama and Yami, whose eclipse in Mazda-worship has been attributed to overtones of pride, violent animal sacrifice, and aspirations for the godhead, were replaced by the couple whose disregard of divine commands is reminiscent of Near Eastern prototypes (Yasna 9: 4–5, 32: 8; Yasht 5: 25–26, 15: 15–16, 17: 28–31, 19: 31–38; Videvdad 2: 1–42; Pahlavi Rivayat Accompanying the Dadestan i Denig 31: 1–10, 31a: 1–3, 31b: 1–8).[3] The non-Iranian, ancient Near Eastern, origin of this leitmotif was not lost on artists later on during Muslim rule. One of them depicted Angra Mainyu as an old man tempting the primal couple to taste a pomegranate or quince and thereby gain knowledge and immortality. First Mashyana and then Mashya were presented as having succumbed to temptation (figure 2). A primordial scene was created, visually, through a cave-like setting. The primal nature of the first humans, like the spiritual nature of Angra Mainyu, was depicted via halos. But the evil spirit is dressed in a black robe—a symbolical representation of his nature which would have been a powerful visual cue for Mazdeans whose theology associated all forms of darkness with the realm of evil.

The medieval visual image represents a variation in the use of food as a metaphor for sex and the Fall, for according to the Bundahishn this couple consumed milk and meat instead of the proverbial pomegranate that was illustrated (14: 18–21). Perhaps some medieval Zoroastrian notions that consumption of flesh was sinful, as it necessitated the killing of animals which could effect cosmic order, were augmented by similar beliefs in Manichaeism and then introduced into the story (M 7984; Boyce 1975: 72; compare Widengren 1983b: 979). Much like Adam and Eve, Mashya and Mashyana attempted to conceal their nakedness in both the Pahlavi account and the miniature painting. Unlike Eve, Mashyana was not the sole instigator or perpetrator of the first chaotic deed—so she shared the blame and the punishment. However, her ostensible haste in worshipping the sources of disorder for a second time served medieval magi and laymen as a vivid representation of feminine inability to obey divine law and wishes. The account, following its Judeo-Christian precursor, also served to highlight the disasters that were thought to occur when the female gender was permitted to exercise authority and make decisions—in this case a problem supposedly inherited by all generations of humans thereafter (compare Clark 1986: 31).[4]

Disobedience and error of judgment that resulted in veneration of the source of disorder were exploited as examples of women's susceptibility to evil, temptation, and harmful action. The Chidag Handarz i Poryotkeshan, "Select Counsels of the Ancient Sages," a ninth-century C.E. Pahlavi catechism specifically forbids Zoroastrians from confusing evil with good and, as a result, worshipping entities regarded as demonic (4). The Bundahishn records that due to Mashyane's sinful deeds, the forces of evil prevented the couple from procreating for fifty years thus stifling yet another task ordained by Ahura Mazda as necessary for sustaining cosmic order (Bundahishn 14: 29–30; compare Chidag Handarz i Poryotkeshan 5, 50).

Woman's fertility makes her guarantor of human and cosmic continuity, the link between family, people, and the progress of time (Lincoln 1981: 96, 103–104, 107). By impeding her own fertility and procreative function, from an allegorical viewpoint, Mashyana stifled creation, threatened the continuity of humanity, and violated universal harmony. One error led to another, drawing the first couple further away from god. Similarly, any evil act due to female imperfection and weakness is believed to blaze a trail of chaos. In essence, men endowed the mythical primeval woman, and through her most mortal women, with qualities and inadequacies they beheld in all people. The aggregate image of the feminine thus constructed was then projected upon women and exploited as a gauge by which to denounce the female. This development was, as suggested above, not unique to Mashyana. Weakness, it was thought, resulted in disharmony whenever a woman acted independently. Belief in such chaos, in turn, reinforces the nexus of imperfection and evil.

Of course, Mazdaism, as other religions, does not condemn all women as personifications of evil. Rather, it exploits the duality ascribed to women (compare Clark 1986: 24–25). Yet, overall, there is a tendency to regard women as weak in their denial of evil and strong through their espousing of wickedness. This image of women, distorted though it may be, was captured in Greek historiography on the Achaemenians with noblewomen such as Atossa or Utautha, the wife of Darius I among other rulers and the mother of Xerxes or Xshayarsha I (ruled 486–465 B.C.E.), Amestris or Amastri, one of Xerxes I's queens, and queen Parysatis, the mother of Artaxerxes II and Cyrus or Kurush the Younger (d. 401 B.C.E.) coming to be depicted as despotic, scheming, treacherous, cruel, and seductive—the alleged sources of turmoil and social discord (see further Sancisi-Weerdenburg 1993: 21, 23–25, 27–28).

Later, medieval fears surrounding supposedly malevolent consequences of female imperfection were framed in sayings attributed to Adurbad the son of Maraspand, a leading exponent of Zoroastrian orthodoxy, referred to previously. Perceiving women as morally and intellectually questionable, untrustworthy, and quick to sin, this priest is said to have urged pious men to "tell no secrets to a woman lest your toiling be fruitless," and "not place your trust in women so that you have no reason to come to shame and to repent" (Pahlavi Texts 59: 11, 149: 48–49). Similar notions are professed in the Handarz i Oshnar, "Counsels of Oshnar," a Pahlavi collection of sayings that date from the reign of Xusro I but were accredited to a legendary Kayanian sage. According to the text: "A woman should be regarded as very disagreeable, [although] it is proper to be friendly with one's own virtuous wife" (26–27). Due to women's ascribed penchant for impiety, another saying in the same work claims that "it is not possible to pronounce any opinion on a woman until she is dead" (28). Sentiments recorded in the text Xusro ud Redag complement the passages cited above. In response to the king's question about which type of woman was the best, the page allegedly answered, "that woman is the best who in her disposition is man's friend [and] who does not speak indecent words to men" (95–96). It seems amiability and submissiveness coupled with knowing each gender's religiously-assigned role and purpose in the world, in addition to physical beauty, were the qualities sought by men in women.

New Persian literature continued such images of women even when Zoroastrianism's domination of Iranian culture was in decline. The Seljuk vizier Nezam al-Molk (d. 1092 C.E.) wrote in his Seyasat nama, "Book of Government," also known as the Seyar al-moluk, "Rules for Kings," that "women do not have full intelligence" (226). He then went on to cite examples of female inadequacy (Spellberg 1988: 111–114). The ever popular epic Vis o Ramin presented the heroine Vis as an individual who possesses "the nature of a sorceress" and "will not become tame" (27, 80). Iranian influences may also be reflected in the mysteries of Mithras. While it is appears that cult arose not within the boundaries of Iran but on the frontier of Iran and Asia Minor between the first century B.C.E. and the first century C.E., and then was adopted and disseminated by the Roman military, it bears Iranian influences (Colpe 1983; Ulansey 1989). The mysteries developed into a male cult to which even slaves were admitted but from which women, labeled hyenas, were excluded (Burkert 1987: 7, 42–43, 52, 149). There is no evidence that women ever served as priestesses, initiates, or even donors (Cumont 1956: 173; 1975: 199, 210; see further Gordon 1996: III, 98, IV, 70–71, V, 42–63). A belief even arose that the divinity Mithras was born from a rock and despised women—hence no feminine aspect should threaten the perfect cosmic order that Mithras had set into motion (Colpe 1983: 853–856; Burkert 1987: 106–107, 169). Likewise, Armenian Christian notions of women as weak willed and evil would be derived partially from a confluence of Zoroastrian and Christian ideas of the feminine and the female (compare Alishan 1989: 88, 90–91).

Feminine imperfection as a harbinger of doom has been symbolized throughout the history of Mazda-worship by the Pairika or Parig, a class of witches. Particularly feared among these witches was Duzhyairya (Gray 1929: 205; Malandra 1983: 141; Panaino 1996). She was said to be the maleficent force of bad omens and famine, "who can completely rupture the life-force of the entire material world" (Yasht 8: 54). The Achaemenian monarch Darius I entreated Ahura Mazda to save his empire from this chaotic menace: "protect this land from famine" (Persepolis inscription d: 18–20). The blight allegedly portended by Duzhyairya could only be overcome by Tishtrya, "Sirius," who provides "requital from the enmity of the witch ... whom evil-speaking people call the 'good crop.' [He] shackles [her] with insurmountable double, triple, and multiple bonds, like a thousand men with the utmost physical strength were to shackle a single man" (Yasht 8: 51, 55). Considered equally dangerous was Mush Parig, "Rat Witch," who, in medieval Zoroastrian demonology, opposed the sun and sought to envelope the earth in darkness (Yasna 16: 8, 68: 8; Bundahishn 5: 4–5; see also Gray 1929: 210; Boyce 1989: 86). Mush and other Pairikas were associated with human sorceresses (Yasna 9: 18; Yasht 1: 6; Videvdad 20: 10). Witches were assumed to blaze across the night sky in the form of meteors (Yasht 8: 8), like their Indian counterparts. Medieval Zoroastrian abhorrence for these spirits was eventually transmitted to Manichaeism (M 7 II, M 1202; Boyce 1975: 106, 189).

Pairikas, although feared, could be smitten if men recite holy words or light sacred fires—i.e., perform ritual acts that presumably reinforce cosmic order and righteousness (Yasht 3: 5, 11: 6, Videvdad 8: 80). These witches supposedly are also no match for the male divine spirits Tishtrya or Tishtar and Mithra (Yasht 8: 8, 44, 10: 26, 34). Armenian folk beliefs, based on Iranian ones, also depicted these female spirits as evil (J. R. Russell 1987: 449). Witches, it seems, violate the ordained social structure—indeed, they are female entities thought to dwell beyond the rules of god and man. Armed with dangerous powers and in alliance with the devil, they are thought to prey upon innocent and pure men—leading their victims outside the framework of religious order (Douglas 1982: 107, 113–114, 118–119). Like a demoness, a witch may exhibit unbridled lust and it was feared that men, try as they might, may not be able to withstand the onslaught of disorder and, hence, evil that these spirits represent (compare in part Kloppenborg 1995: viii; O'Flaherty 1982: 91, 278). Even children, the earth, and the celestial spheres allegedly were never safe from a witch's evil so devotees feared she may spread chaos by kidnapping a child, withholding rain, or extinguishing the sun. Yet by the late Middle Ages and early modern times, Pairikas were undergoing a gradual process of rehabilitation—much like the demoness of sloth Bushyasta—being transformed into cunning, yet still fairly noxious, entities as dualism began to attenuate within Zoroastrian doctrine (Christensen 1941: 14–15; Asmussen 1982: 115–117).

Religious systems that view evil as an attack on a structured universe include defilement of the sacred as a goal of the devil. Defilement produces impurity and, consequently, imperfection in the realms of ethical and cosmic order (Ricoeur 1969: 25–46). Defilement, impurity, and imperfection give rise to the notion of pollution through contact with evil and disorder (Douglas 1969: 2–8, 35, 40; Choksy 1989a: xxiv–xxvii). An important sign of imperfection in the dualistic Zoroastrian religious cosmos is pollution (Weber 1956/1978: I, 479). The faith systematically classified all creatures and things along the concepts of purity and impurity. Mazdean doctrine equated pollution with disorder, and then associated it with death and the feminine from the earliest period of the community's formation. As mentioned earlier, Zoroastrians believe that all the creations were produced perfect and pure by Ahura Mazda (Denkard 251: 12–13; Chidag Handarz i Poryotkeshan 10–14). Hence, pollution came to be a symbol of disorder in creatures, and this imperfection was attributed in ancient and medieval times to Angra Mainyu, demons, and demonesses (Videvdad 20: 3, 22: 2; Bundahishn 4: 15). Humans, as the foremost of god's creations, were expected to abjure pollution.

Pollution, as a manifestation of spiritual and corporeal imperfection, was personified in the form of the female Nasush, "Corpse [demoness]," believed to attack all the material creations of Ahura Mazda—earth, water, fire, metal, plants, animals, and humans (Gray 1929: 211; Boyce 1989: 86–87, 300). Nasush is regarded as the demoness who causes death, decay, and pollution in corpses, excrement, and people—especially, women. Her physical description was first recorded in the Young Avesta as "the form of a fly, disgusting, with crooked knees, protruding buttocks, [and covered] with unlimited spots like the most horrible, noxious, creature" (Videvdad 7: 2, 9: 26). Centuries later, in the Farziyat nama, a New Persian text, she was still described as "the most impudent, constantly polluting, and deceptive of all the demonic spirits" (10). Her genesis may be linked with that of the Armenian ghoul Shiraki who also moved through the gloom in the shape of a fly (J. R. Russell 1987: 445). Zoroastrian religious texts—from the Avesta to contemporary New Persian and Gujarati exegeses—outline rules that devotees are urged to follow in order to safeguard themselves and the entire world from Nasush. Such stipulations are thought to maintain and even recreate the purity of order in the face of the impurity of chaos (Choksy 1989a: 7–10).

Impurity which originates from this female demon supposedly causes two major categories of pollution: that in corpses and excrement, and that in women (Malandra 1983: 162). When an animal or human dies, the corpse or any portion of it is said to be immediately polluted by Nasush (Choksy 1989a: 17–18). Carrion is always in the highest state of impurity, unless it has been ritually purified and the demoness driven away. The demoness' defiling power was said in the Avesta to be directly proportional to the spiritual good-standing of the individual whose corpse she pollutes (Videvdad 5: 28, 35–38). A medieval commentary stated this is because triumph over the corpse of a righteous man requires all her might, and, in turn, the polluted flesh becomes capable of spreading pollution widely (Gizistag Abalish, "[Book about] the Accursed Abalish," 6: 3). In the case of an unrighteous person, little evil is thought to be needed to overwhelm the body and pollute it; hence the impure flesh cannot spread much disorderly pollution in its own turn (Gizistag Abalish 6: 3;

Persian Revayats 1: 136). Excrement comprises all body fluids and refuse once these have been expelled, discharged, or separated from the body—i.e., once separated from the structured unit of each person. Skin, saliva, breath, nails, hair, urine, feces, semen, and blood are encompassed by this category, and all may be defiled by Nasush outside the body. Deliberate pollution of the elements and living creatures through contact with carrion and excrement is considered a grievous sin punishable by the torments of hell. Even involuntary pollution of the creations is an impious deed, for it spreads impurity in the world, thereby furthering disorder and evil at the expense of the religiously ordained righteous order of the cosmos (Choksy 1989a: 10–16, 18–19).

Fear of pollution caused by the Corpse demoness dictated elaborate purification rituals, purity rites, and daily practices incumbent upon all Mazda-worshipers. Corpses had to be exposed to the elements—originally on dry, desolate ground, later in funerary towers. Only after exposure and desiccation did pollution supposedly cease. Then the bones could be placed in repositories. Alternately, dead bodies could be placed in rock tombs or stone caskets—for Zoroastrians believed, based on their creation myth, that stone was a creation of Ahura Mazda's which evil could not penetrate or escape from once enclosed. Burial in the earth, disposal in water, and cremation were thought to pollute the sacred elements of earth, water, and fire (Videvdad 6: 10–11, 7: 25–27, 49–51)—as mentioned previously. Elaborate precautions had to be observed by corpse bearers, usually men, so that the demoness symbolically would not spring upon them from the corpse. Many of these practices continued in excruciating detail through the seventeenth century C.E. (Persian Revayats 1: 78, 82). Attenuation of belief in this female demon's power has combined with secular and urban trends among contemporary Zoroastrians, resulting in exposure of corpses now being restricted to Parsi communities in a few cities including Bombay and Karachi. Burial is the norm among both urban and rural Irani Zoroastrians, Parsi Zoroastrians in Indian and Pakistani towns and villages, and Zoroastrians in Sri Lanka, Europe, Canada, the United States of America, and Australia, as already outlined in chapter two.[5]

Several rituals serve to purify living Zoroastrians from the symbolic blight of Nasush—thereby reasserting religious order. The Padyab, performed daily, reestablishes ritual purity prior to prayer and meals, and after bodily functions (Choksy 1989a: 53–62). Nahn rituals are undergone during rites of passage to ensure purification from Nasush prior to initiation into the faith and marriage, and after childbirth (Choksy 1989a: 62–71). The Barashnum i no shab, an elaborate ceremony conducted over nine days and nights, purifies devotees—in modern time particularly priests—from the impurity caused by Nasush through contact with carrion (Choksy 1989a: 23–52). Precautions and purity rites in daily life once surrounded the clipping of hair, paring of nails, and performance of all bodily functions. Some rites still are employed to prevent breath and saliva from contaminating ritual implements or the sacred fires, and to protect personal property from pollution by this demoness (Choksy 1989a: 80–88, 104–107). Likewise, rites used to be practiced to safeguard sexual intercourse and prevent impurity which may arise from the discharge of semen outside human bodies (Choksy 1989a: 88–94).

Bleeding was regarded as another sign of an attack by the Corpse demoness. Blood, like semen, is not regarded as impure itself, in Mazdean theology, while confined within the body. But any flow of blood outside the body affects purity because it symbolically violates the idealized physical state of humans and places devotees of Ahura Mazda at the mercy of Nasush (Boyce 1989: 307; Choksy 1989a: 94–95). Fear of blood, sex, and the procreative function of women resulted in the feminine and the female coming to be linked to the supernatural. In particular, blood and procreation were associated with spiritual forces viewed as potentially polluting and, hence, disruptive to men and divinities (see also Savramis 1974: 13–14, 44, 58; Elliott 1999: 7). Menstruation, through its links with blood and pollution, was thought to pose a grave threat to the pure cosmic order constructed by divine spirits and men (Videvdad 1: 18–19; 16: 1–12). By the medieval era, belief that menstruation was linked to impurity and, hence, evil had resulted in a myth woven into the faith's cosmogony (compare Choksy 1988a: 74, 77–78). Menstruation, that legend claimed, originated when Jahika, the Whore demoness, revived Angra Mainyu at the beginning of time: "Angra Mainyu was comforted finally, arose from that stupor, and kissed the

Whore's face, [and] the pollution which is termed menstruation appeared from her" (Bundahishn 4: 5). Myth and physiology combined in Zoroastrian beliefs and practices that relate to menstruation. Monthly discharge of blood was attributed to lust produced in women by Jahika. The ritual pollution that apparently results from this discharge was deemed Nasush's handiwork. Hence, the religion implied that two female demons and all mortal women unite to violate male ritual purity and render men unfit for resisting evil. So rites were formulated to cleanse women after menstruation (see further Choksy 1989a: 97–99).

Childbirth is regarded as essential for reproducing the Mazdeans necessary to combat disorder. While the female divine spirits that women are supposed to emulate were not said to marry or have offspring, the problem created through this disjunction between spiritual and corporeal was bridged by childbirth being viewed as an extension of Ahura Mazda's creative function vital for the eventual triumph of order over disorder (see also Kloppenborg 1995: viii). Moreover, Spenta Armaiti was regarded as the spiritual mother of humanity, just as Ahura Mazda was thought of as the spiritual father: "Ahura Mazda replied, 'This is Spenta Armaiti my daughter, my house-mistress of paradise, and the mother of creation'" (Pahlavi Rivayat Accompanying the Dadestan i Denig 8: 4). Yet despite the value attributed to reproduction, as in the case of menstruation any bleeding connected to passage of the placenta out of the body after childbirth supposedly results in ritual pollution of the mother by the Corpse demoness within the religious system. So rites evolved to purify women after childbirth, reestablishing the ritual purity thought to be so vital for proper functioning of the universe inhabited by men and divinities (Choksy 1989a: 99–101).

Zoroastrians still strive to control the pollution that is presumed to arise from Nasush by performing daily rites of purity, occasionally undergoing purification rituals, and protecting the sacred creations of god from impurity (Choksy 1989a: 53–62, 78–94). Likewise, they seek to counter feminine imperfection signified by this demoness through recitation of prayers such as the Kem Na Mazda and Srosh Baj (Yasht i Dron dedicated to Sraosha) which call upon male divine beings, Ahura Mazda and Sraosha in particular, to vanquish death, decay, and impurity. Light is believed to be essential for victory in the battle against imperfection, impurity, and pollution. Hence, rites to expel the Corpse demoness usually are conducted during the daytime. Then, another masculine image, the sun, can be summoned to shore up male devotees.

The imperfection, impurity, and mortality inherent in Pairikas and in Nasush may be contrasted with the perfection, purity, and regenerative powers ascribed to the two beneficent immortals Haurvatat, "Integrity, Wholeness, and hence Perfection" and Ameretat, "Immortality, Rejuvenation," both female in the Avesta. The notions of perfection and immortality were captured by the religion's medieval theology through homologies between Haurvatat, Ameretat, water, and plants which relate macrocosm to microcosm (see Bundahishn 3: 18–19; Supplementary Texts to the Shayest ne Shayest 15: 5–6). In the case of Haurvatat and water, the homology is based on the idea of completeness and inseparability, the ability to flow together present in fluids and, allegorically, in the continuity of life. The notion of wholeness encompassed by the beneficent immortal is not restricted to the physical realm but extends to spiritual perfection (Choksy 1989a: 120). Immortality present in Ameretat is linked in a homology to plants through the concept of incessant growth and seasonal rejuvenation (Choksy 1989a: 84, 117). It came to be believed that men may gain the assistance of these two female divinities through self-control (Boyce 1989: 221). Haurvatat provides health, Ameretat grants long life. They protect water and plants, thus sustaining life (Boyce 1977: 46, 51–52; 1985b). Hence, they are thought to be capable of countering thirst and hunger inflicted by Duzhyairya (Yasht 19: 96), while possessing healing powers to restore well-being and thereby ensure a return to appropriate states of religiocosmic order (compare Yasht 8: 47). Together, Haurvatat and Ameretat, health and long life, symbolically resist the onslaught of evil and uphold righteousness. This resistance, in turn, leads to perfection and immortality of body and soul for humanity it is believed (Yasna 34: 10–11). As feminine divine beings, they represent medieval Zoroastrian notions of "bountifulness, perfect thought, and completeness" that are said to result in society's "good protection through wholeness and immortality" (Denkard 415:

14–15, 416: 1–2).

Originally, in the Gathas, Zarathushtra had referred to Haurvatat and Ameretat as benefits obtained from Ahura Mazda (Kellens 2000: 5, 18, 48). So when the Young Avestan texts were incorporated into nascent Mazdaism, Haurvatat and Ameretat came to be symbolized by sacrificial offerings—the liquid and plant portions of materials proffered by the devotional poet and by other supplicants to divine beings (Humbach 1991: I, 92–94). Hence, they represented initially non-corporeal benefits and, later, material offerings—in both cases, passive commodities. It should not be surprising, therefore, that these two were regarded as more quiescent and of lower ranking than their masculine or neuter counterparts within the canonical hierarchy of Amesha Spentas in the Young Avestan texts (Narten 1982: 98–102; Kellens 2000: 61–62). Yet, they had eschatological functions at the ritual center of a symmetrical arrangement of Amesha Spentas bounded by Spenta Mainyu and Ahura Mazda (Windfuhr 1976: 244–250, 273–286). Therefore, by the Middle Ages, and with the loss of grammatical gender in the Pahlavi language, Haurvatat and Ameretat came to be regarded as neuter, almost masculine, entities—unlike Spenta Armaiti who remained feminine (Boyce 1989: 205–206). Perhaps that gender shift reflects not only a linguistic change but also an unconscious transition based on the aggressive, almost male, roles gradually attributed by the medieval magi to Haurvatat and Ameretat in combating evil and ensuring salvation.

The feminine is omnipresent even after death—which came to be regarded as another disruption in the cycles of religious order and goodness—in forms wrought by the deeds and illusions of men. Zoroastrian tales of an afterlife in heaven and hell were popular during late antiquity and the Middle Ages (see further Gignoux 1968). Such stories served as warnings to women to make no attempts to disrupt society or to harm men. Those accounts were also didactic for men—cautioning against evil directly and feminine wiles indirectly. An early vision was attributed to the late-third-century C.E. chief magus Kirdir who had it inscribed, perhaps for those who were literate to read and recount to the illiterate, in public settings (Back 1978: 384–487; Skjærvø 1983; Gignoux 1991: 40–45, 48–52). Kirdir's tale is the earliest surviving description, in any religion, whose date was fixed—in stone—unlike manuscript accounts by early Christians and Muslims which would have been recopied and revised (on those descriptions see Daley 1999a, 1999b).

The most popular such reverie was titled the Arda Wiraz namag. It was copied many times not only in the Pahlavi language but later in New Persian and Gujarati, and manuscripts were illustrated with miniature paintings. The account was intended to augment scripture with vivid, supposedly firsthand, recounting of the pleasures of paradise and the trails of hell. It may have been hoped that, through exposure to the story and illustrations, literate devotees could be convinced to uphold righteousness and in turn would describe the cautionary scenes to other individuals who were illiterate or had no access to the text and art. According to that medieval tale, in heaven Wiraz encountered "souls of those women, submissive to control, who had regarded their husbands as lords, who had practiced acquiescence and conformity [in] obedience and reverence toward their husbands and lords, [and] had abstained from sin" (13: 4).

In illustrations, the souls of women in heaven customarily sit in passive poses—occasionally engaging in conversation but rarely displaying any emotions (figure 3). Their existence in heaven, at least in visual form, appears to have been conceived as insular to the feminine gender. They were separated from sexuality, impurity, and chaos—having no contact with members of the masculine gender so that the spiritual order of both genders would not be threatened in any way or for any reason. On the other hand, the souls of righteous men are not simply lumped together into a single category. Rather, in the Arda Wiraz namag—as in other Mazdean accounts of the afterlife—they were discussed in terms of social ranks, occupations, and categories of good deeds performed. In accompanying artwork, they were depicted partaking of paradisiacal merriment (figure 4) or engaged in other pursuits, like reading, deemed appropriate for members of the masculine gender. Their female companions are virginal female spirits rather than the souls of deceased mortal women. So, again, gender separation seems to have prevailed—with art reflecting socioreligious norms.

Within the murky depths of hell, Arda Wiraz supposedly witnessed punishment of women's souls for violating religious codes

FIGURE 3. REWARD OF FEMALE SOULS IN HEAVEN. Illustration from an Arda Wiraz namag manuscript. Middle seventeenth century C.E. *Courtesy of a private collection.*

FIGURE 4. REWARD OF MALE SOULS IN HEAVEN. Illustration from an Arda Wiraz namag manuscript. Middle seventeenth century C.E. *Courtesy of a private collection.*

while incarnate (figure 5). Indeed, pain-filled afterlives were believed to await women who practiced idolatry and sorcery (like Xnathaiti and Pairikas) (25: 1–3), committed adultery and sexual profligacy (following Jahika) (24: 1–4), violated ritual purity (with Nasush) (34: 1–3, 76: 1–5), or disobeyed men and caused strife (like Drug and Asrushti) (26: 1–3). Their suffering would only cease after time ended. Such literary and visual depictions would have reminded women of the need to remain virtuous and submissive—fulfilling the familial and devotional duties prescribed to them (compare Rose 1989: 30).

Duality ascribed to the feminine also was linked with the soul's fate at death in another fashion. By medieval times, Zoroastrians had come to believe that after an individual dies his or her mortal soul stays by its corpse's head for three days and nights. When dawn arrives on the fourth day, this soul is led to Chinvato-Peretu, "bridge of the compiler," to undergo judgment based on good and bad actions while incarnate.[6] Thereupon, the soul encounters its Daena or Den, "conscience," in very specific female forms (figure 6). Originally venerated as an abstract notion, the Daena even had been included in early lists of Amesha Spentas within the Old Avestan liturgical corpus (consult Kellens 2000: 20, 53–54, 60). According to the Gathas, the soul of a righteous man, "who has allied his Daena with good thoughts" will be led into paradise for "heaven shall be the future possession of him who becomes a truthful person" (Yasna 49: 5, 31: 20). On the other hand, it is believed that the soul of an evil man will be tossed into hell. In hell, its companionship supposedly includes the "Daena for a long age of darkness, foul food, and woe" (Yasna 31: 20, 46: 11; see also Widengren 1983a; Lankarany 1985; Vahman 1985; Shaki 1996).

The gender of Daenas is an important issue (Lommel 1930: 150–151; Duchesne-Guillemin 1966: 19–21). In the Hadhoxt nask, a late Young Avestan eschatological text of which only fragments are extant, it was recorded that a righteous man's soul would be greeted by its Daena "as a beautiful girl, radiant, well-formed, statuesque, having prominent breasts, a shapely body, noble, of high birth, fifteen years old in appearance—the most attractive of individuals" (2: 22–23; compare Videvdad 19: 30). Similar descriptions of celestial

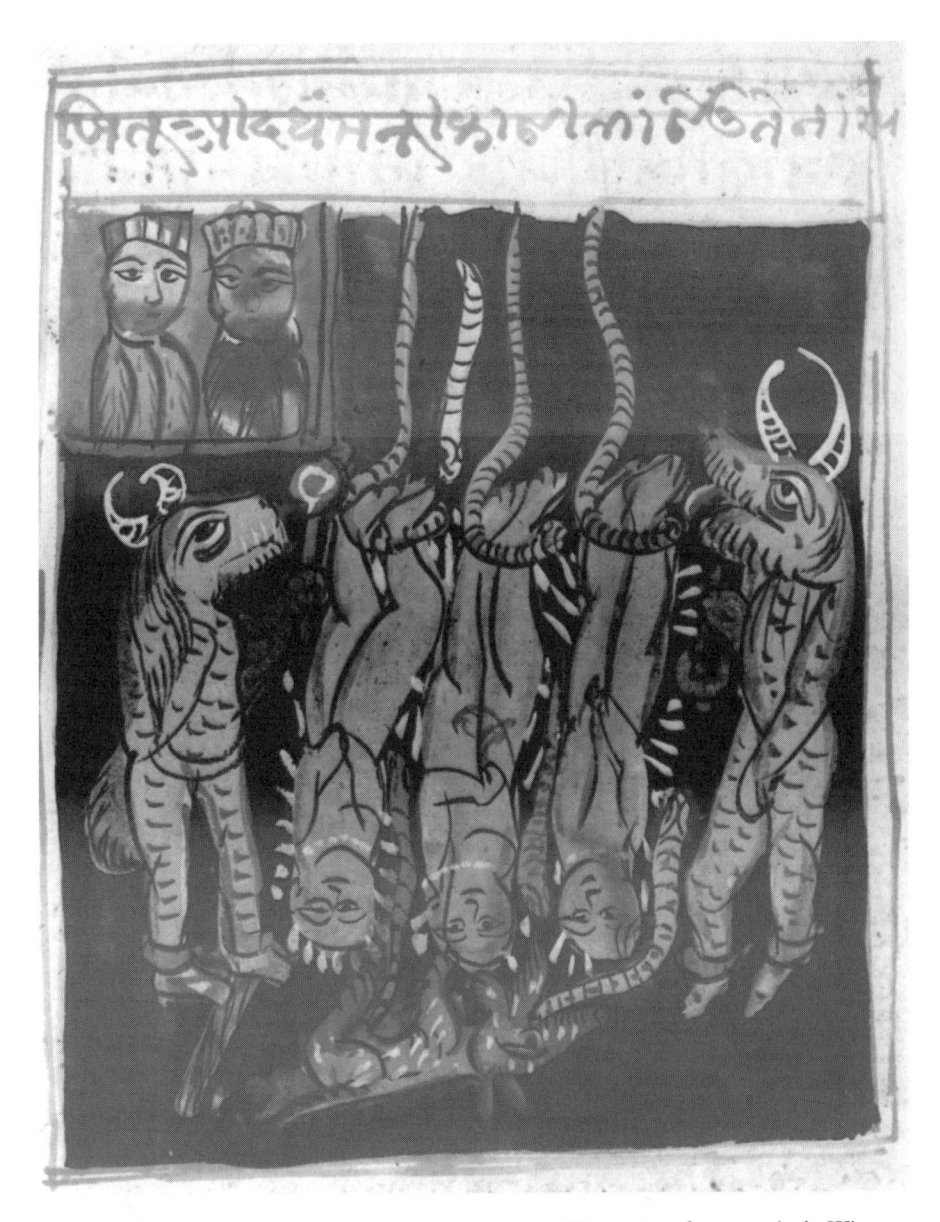

FIGURE 5. PUNISHMENT OF FEMALE SOULS IN HELL. Illustration from an Arda Wiraz namag manuscript. Middle seventeenth century C.E. *Courtesy of a private collection.*

FIGURE 6. A MALE SOUL ENCOUNTERS ITS DAENA. Illustration from an Arda Wiraz namag manuscript. Middle seventeenth century C.E. *Courtesy of a private collection.*

· WEAKNESS, IMPERFECTION, DEATH ·   71

FIGURE 7. SASANIAN SILVER BOWL IMAGES OF DAENAS. Fifth or sixth century C.E. *Courtesy of a private collection.*

virgins were incorporated into medieval pious literature, like the Menog i Xrad where it was written that after death, at the time of judgment, a pious man's "own good deeds will come toward him in the form of a girl, more beautiful and attractive than any woman in the world" (2: 125–126; compare Arda Wiraz namag 4: 9; Bundahishn 30: 14)—a reward, it seems, crafted from male desires. Again, miniature paintings in manuscripts of the Arda Wiraz namag vividly illustrated this spiritual encounter—depicting scales for judgment, heavenly beings, the Daena who was sometimes shown veiled to indicate modesty, and the male soul (figure 6). This artistic tradition was carried over to more secular, occasionally highly-erotic, representations on silver bowls (figure 7; compare Azarpay 1976: especially 37–38, 42–47) and stamp seals (Gnoli 1993: 81–82, and figures 1–3). So the attractive Daena became a symbol of the good life—including sensuality, music, and bountifulness—after death for pious Mazda-worshipers, but a manifestation of suffering for irreligious persons. It should also be noted that the good Daena's description in both literature and art has many striking similarities to those of Aredwi Sura Anahita.[7] Perhaps, the image of Anahita as the divine spirit who granted boons was symbolized as the heavenly Daena who satisfied the every wish of pious male human spirits in heaven.

The soul of a Zoroastrian man who has been damned at the

judgment, however, is said to be met by its Daena in the countenance of a hag: "It beheld its own Daena and its deeds in the form of the Whore demoness, naked and decrepit, with crooked knees, protruding buttocks, [and covered] with unlimited spots like the most horrible noxious creature" (Arda Wiraz namag 17: 9; compare Menog i Xrad 2: 167–178; Bundahishn 30: 18). In addition to the direct reference to Jahika, it is important to note resemblances between descriptions of the evil Daena and the demoness Nasush. Daenas, heavenly and demonic, beautiful and hideous, are discussed further in a late medieval text written in New Persian titled the Saddar Bondahesh, "[Book of] Primal Creation written in One Hundred Chapters," (99: 1–6, 16–20). Thereafter, the New Persian and Gujarati Zoroastrian literature omits all mention of them—unless such texts are merely translations of Avestan and Pahlavi documents.

Attractive and unattractive Daenas were depicted in the art of medieval Mazdeans living in Central Asia, albeit in Sinophile form (Grenet and Guangda 1998: 175–179 and figure 1). Thus, not surprisingly, Manichaean imagery from Central Asia of spirits encountered after death is reminiscent of the Zoroastrian Daena. The soul of an electus (dendar) is met by a "maiden of light" while that of a sinner encounters a "lying, hairy, grisly she-demon" (Pavry 1929: 46–48; Boyce 1975: 7–8).[8] Islamic belief, perhaps also echoing Iranian motifs, presents paradise as a garden where the pious are rewarded with Huris (Hur) or beautiful, young, virginal spirits whose eyes were compared to pearls. The Huris are represented as "modest" feminine beings "whom neither man nor genie has touched before" (Qur'an 37: 48–49, 44: 54, 52: 20, 55: 56–58, 72, 56: 22, 36, 78: 33). As in medieval Zoroastrianism, Muslim heavenly females are reserved for male believers whose every need they supposedly fulfill (Smith and Haddad 1981: 89, 164–166, 178).

Only Daenas who meet the souls of men have been discussed because the ancient and medieval theological literature of Mazdaism provides little evidence that women's souls encounter Daenas—although Zarathushtra himself, in his devotional poems, spoke of female souls crossing the spiritual bridge on their journey to heaven or hell (Yasna 46: 10). The faith's patriarchal hierarchy, as it developed, directed ancient and medieval devotees' focus on the distinctions between order and disorder as good versus evil by connecting it to a dichotomy represented by the feminine in the afterlife. Male righteousness in life was believed to be rewarded by the heavenly female; male wickedness was believed to be punished by the demonic female (Choksy 1998: 256–261). Only in popular belief of modern times has it become the norm to assume that women too will encounter their own Daenas, although indirect allusions to women's souls meeting with Daenas may have existed even earlier (see further Gnoli 1993; Panaino 1997). But scant reference is ever made now to the gender of these spiritual manifestations of human deeds. Thus, gender-specific identification has declined during the twentieth century C.E., in relation to beliefs surrounding the afterlife of human souls as the community attempts to disassociate itself from a ritualistic, gender-differential, past when weakness, imperfection, and suffering in both life and afterlife were linked to feminine disorder and disharmony.

Essentially, in Mazdean belief, correct performance of actions—especially ritual ones—provides the *mizhda*, "recompense," by which righteous performers or ashavans ensure their mortal souls are received into the abode of the divinities after death. On the other hand, as already discussed, the souls of those individuals or dregvants whose actions are incorrect will be doomed to an ignoble existence in the abode of the Daevas (Yasna 28: 11, 49: 10–11). So Zoroastrian tenets and rites symbolically depict the processes that link life to afterlife, genesis to conclusion. In other words, cosmogony and eschatology represent the beginning and the end of a linear process connected in the material universe by appropriate liturgies and rituals (compare Kellens 2000: xv, 102–103). Within that scheme of existence, one point of nexus between the corporeal and spiritual realms supposedly is Chinvato-Peretu. Earliest Iranian mythology relating to this bridge seems to have regarded Yima as its builder, piling up the stones that spanned the space between the earth and the hereafter (Kellens 2000: xv, 13–14, 98). Thus reflecting a common Indo-Iranian heritage, Yima—like the Vedic Yama—was presumed to have charted the path to an afterlife. Most interestingly, it appears that even access to the divine spiritual abode was paved by a masculine figure.

As described in this chapter, Zoroastrian cosmogony and spirituality created a scheme wherein disorder—with its links to evil—was ascribed, in part, to the feminine gender metaphorically from the inception of human existence. Additionally, Zoroastrian theology and ritual cover many aspects of each devotee's life—from birth to death and the afterlife—with special focus on countering the chaos allegedly generated by the feminine gender. Ranging from the images of Mashyana to the Daena of impious men, and from the notions of Pairikas to Nasush, the Mazdean desire to control and structure the religious universe impacted on the lives and statuses of men and women in different manners.

CHAPTER FIVE

Society in Antiquity & the Middle Ages

Extant records from the first large-scale, Mazdean or Zoroastrian society, that of Iran under the Achaemenian dynasty, indicate women did play a wide variety of roles.[1] Their presence is attested in royal settings as queens, other noblewomen, concubines, and slaves, in familial settings as wives, daughters, and household workers and in a wide range of workplaces—from the market to building sites. According to evidence from the Persepolis Fortification Tablets, dating to the fifth century B.C.E., non-elite women and girls served as artisans, cooks, and textile workers (PF 864–865, 999; see further Lewis 1990: 2–3; Brosius 1996: 146–180). Most women had a wide range of legal rights and responsibilities under Achaemenian civil law. They could own movable and immovable property, and exchange, bequeath, inherit, lease, sell, and trade such items—for example, Irdabama whose property was extensive (Brosius 1996: 125, 127, 129–144). They could enter into contracts and attest contractual documents with their own seals, but could not serve as witnesses in their own right (compare Dandamayev and Lukonin 1989: 124–125). Yet, simultaneously, they seem to have been regarded under both state laws and religious codes as the property of men (see further Balcer 1993: 309–310).

Much of the specific information available centers on female members of the nobility, who traveled extensively and were present at official events (Brosius 1996: 84, 87–97).[2] Herodotus briefly wrote about Mandane, daughter of the last Median king Astyages or Rshtivaiga (ruled 585–549 B.C.E.) and mother of the Achaemenian dynastic founder Cyrus or Kurush II (ruled 549–530 B.C.E.), in reference to Cyrus' birth story (I: 107–108). Herodotus (II: 1) also recorded the presence of Cassandane, one of Cyrus II's wives whose memory was preserved, it seems, largely in relation to her having legitimized his rule over Media through marriage and having borne him five children (Boyce 1983: 59). Another wife of Cyrus II's was said to have been Astyages' daughter Amytis or Umaiti (Schmitt 1985a).

Atossa, daughter of Cyrus II, consanguineously married by her brothers Cambyses or Kambujiya II (ruled 530–522 B.C.E.) and Bardiya or Smerdis (ruled 522 B.C.E.), perhaps also wed by the usurper Pseudo-Smerdis or Gaumata (ruled 522 B.C.E.), then made a wife of Darius I and thus became the mother of Xerxes I, was much maligned by classical writers for her alleged interference in politics (Herodotus III: 134, VII: 2–4). This negative image, projected on her, seems to reflect Greek stereotypes of the Other, especially the feminine, rather than historical realities (Sancisi-Weerdenburg 1993: 23–27, 32–33; Brosius 1996: 105–109; and Wiesehöfer 1996: 79–83, 85; contra Schmitt 1989a). Rather, it appears that her sociopolitical authority derived from her familial, royal heritage which resulted in her transmitting political authority from her father—Cyrus II, who had founded the dynasty—to the men who married her. Artystone or Rtastuna, the youngest daughter of Cyrus II and a sister of Atossa, Artabama perhaps the daughter of Gobryas, Parmys or Parmais the daughter of Bardiya or Smerdis, and possibly Abbamush or Apama (Apame), among others, also were wives of Darius I—linking him to more noble families and thus serving as the means of consolidating political alliances (Herodotus III: 88, IV: 132, 134; see further Boyce 1983: 91, 117; Cook 1983: 25, 33, 74, 135; Schmitt 1987; Wiesehöfer 1996: 68–69, 74, 85). Additional ladies at the royal court during Darius I's reign included Radushdukka, who may have been the king's sister, and Radushnamuya (see further Wiesehöfer 1996: 69, 85). Such marriages, involving the acquisition of large harems, provided this king of kings—like other rulers—with legitimacy and alliances (Balcer 1993: 302–303; Brosius 1996: 38–69, 80–82, 204–206). Darius I himself had daughters named Mandane, Artazostre or Artazaushtri, and Artystone (Herodotus VI: 43; see further Kellens 1987).

Amestris the daughter of Otanes was Xerxes I's wife and, hence, an Achaemenian queen. Like Atossa and other women of the imperial harems, she too was portrayed—probably inaccurately—as crafty and vengeful in classical accounts regarding her dealings with another Achaemenian princess named Artaynte (Herodotus IX: 108–113). Again, her textual representation seems to be a Greek rendering intended as an example of oriental decadence (Sancisi-Weerdenburg 1993: 27–30, 32–33; Brosius 1996: 113; and Wiesehöfer 1996: 79–83, 85; contra Boyce 1983: 173–174, 188; Cook 1983: 135; and Schmitt 1985b, who follow the classical depictions). Likewise, Amytis, a daughter of Xerxes I, also was presented in a negative light by being depicted as sexually promiscuous, and Parysatis, wife of Darius or Darayavahush II Nothus (ruled 423–404 B.C.E.), was presented as a dangerous woman (Brosius 1996: 109–112, 113–116; contra Cook 1983: 16; and Schmitt 1985a, both of whom uncritically accept the classical accounts).

The royal women, and their familial ties, indicate that Iranian belief and social praxis found polygyny fully acceptable—and this practice persisted into modern times until phased out by the Iranian and Parsi Zoroastrians under pressure from Europeans. But polyandry was never permitted. Consanguineous marriages are also attested—for example, between Artaxerxes II and his daughters named Atossa and Amestris, in addition to those by Cambyses II and Bardiya mentioned above (see also Boyce 1982: 220, 284). Little is known about the secular and religious stipulations governing marriages among Mazda-worshipers during the Achaemenian period, though it seems to have occurred shortly after puberty—which was the age at which an individual came to be regarded by the faith as responsible for his or her actions (compare Balcer 1993: 288–294; Wiesehöfer 1996: 85). References in Old Persian inscriptions and classical texts suggest that some royal women may have been literate. Perhaps these elite women also played a role in the education of their daughters and, to a more limited degree since edification of elite males included military training, of their sons (Cook 1983: 69; Wiesehöfer 1996: 79–80, 82).

While these noblewomen were mentioned within familial, political, commercial, and even public contexts—for example, in the

Persepolis Fortification Tablets inscribed with the Elamite language and dating from 509–494 B.C.E. and in the works of classical authors—much remained unwritten about their roles in cultic practice. Most extant seals of queens like Artystone bear secular images (Wiesehöfer 1996: plate 13b). The little textual data available is often unreliable, colored by negative stereotypes such as the tale that queen Amestris offered human sacrifices—a custom not otherwise attested among Iranians generally and Mazdeans specifically then or later—in gratitude to an underworld divinity (Herodotus VII: 114; uncritically accepted by Boyce 1982: 167). However, a chalcedony cylinder seal bears the rare image of an unnamed Achaemenian queen or princess making ritual offerings in front of a fire altar and a female divinity (Spycket 1980: 44, and figure 7).

The jewelry of a noblewoman, dating between the second half of the fifth century and the middle of the fourth century B.C.E. and unearthed at Pasargadae, included fifty-one gold pendants of the Egyptian male divinity Bes (Stronach 1978: 170, 177, plates 154a–b, d). This data suggests that elite Achaemenian women were either not all Mazda-worshipers—as would be expected in cases where harems included women from many different geographical and cultural regions of the empire—or that some Iranian women had assimilated veneration of foreign divinities through cross-cultural contact. Noblewomen, like their male counterparts, seem to have reconciled successfully a range of beliefs and practices. The stone mausoleum at Pasargadae and the rock sepulchers at Naqsh-e Rostam suggest that corpses of Achaemenian monarchs such as Cyrus II and Darius I and of their queens were entombed, probably after being embalmed in wax (Xenophon VIII: VII, 27)—rather than being exposed for mangling and the remains collected thereafter for placement in an ossuary (*astodana*) as done for common folk (Stronach 1987: 24–43, and plates 19–36; Schmidt 1970: 80–102, and plates 37–39, 46–47, 54–55, 62, 69, 74c).[3] Stone symbolically would have enclosed ritual impurity caused by the corpses, thus fulfilling Mazdean funerary stipulations—for example, the vault of the sky is believed to be made of rock to trap chaotic evil within the corporeal world (Wizidagiha i Zadspram 3: 1–4).

It is clear the Achaemenians worshipped Ahura Mazda and other masculine and feminine divinities regarded as subordinate to that god. However, connections between the lives and devotions of women during Achaemenian times are very poorly attested—although such activities must have occurred on a daily basis. For example, the Persepolis Fortification Tablets, while providing much-needed documentation of religiosity during the Achaemenian era, shed very little light on the role of the feminine in Mazda-worship at that time—particularly in connection with female votaries (consult in general Koch 1977). The highly masculine-gendered nature of Mazdean ritual at that time is apparent through seventy-three dated and ninety undated mortars, pestles, plates, and trays made of stone, which were used for pounding of haoma during the Yasna ritual between 479 and 435 B.C.E. Inscriptions in Aramaic on these objects—known to scholars as the Aramaic Ritual Texts from Persepolis—directly provide fascinating sacramental information and indirectly yield a plethora of onomastic, administrative, and economic data. But all the individuals mentioned are men, especially priests and military commanders. Women seem not to have been involved in high liturgies, at least at Persepolis and possibly elsewhere within Iran, offered to the male god Ahura Mazda. Perhaps, this explains why the few images—on items like seals and jewelry—suggest that feminine divinities and non-Iranian divine beings found favor in women's devotions.

Women were not mentioned in Achaemenian royal inscriptions (see further Brosius 1996: 14). Moreover, the depiction of women—nobles and commoners—is conspicuously absent from the imperial art of that empire, especially from the palace reliefs at the major administrative centers of Pasargadae, Persepolis, and Susa (compare Spycket 1980: 43; Cook 1983: 165; Sancisi-Weerdenburg 1993: 22–23). Granted, much of the art that has survived the vicissitudes of time is mainly monumental imperial propaganda. Yet, their absence in the processional scenes like those flanking the apadana or audience hall platform in the royal citadel at Persepolis—where men from many different social ranks, professional occupations, geographic areas, and ethnic groups are depicted—seems to mark a disparity that existed in Achaemenian society between the public roles assigned by custom and religion to men vis-à-vis the private and domestic functions expected of women (contra Brosius 1996: 86). When represented, feminine images appear in less formal settings—as figurines of bronze, ivory, and limestone, small busts of lapis lazuli, limestone, and terra-cotta, rings and plaques of gold, and pendants and scaraboids of semiprecious stone (Spycket 1980: 43–45, and figures 1–2, 4, 6, 8–9; Moorey 1988: plates 59–60, 78b–c; Boardman 2000: 155, 171–172). Textual accounts suggest that additional, non-official images once existed—such as the depiction supposedly commissioned in gold by Darius I of his wife Artystone (Herodotus VII: 69). Men, on the other hand, are commonplace in Achaemenian artworks such as rock and bas reliefs, sculptures, seals, and coins (see numerous plates in Schmidt 1939, 1953–1970; Porada 1965; Stronach 1978). Kings were depicted as warriors, hunters, and votaries. Emissaries, commoners, and servants are shown bearing goods and serving the nobility. Their artistic representations, like their lives, seem to reflect no disjunctions between secular and spiritual spheres of activity—be it receiving defeated foes, slaying wild animals, carrying bowls, transporting livestock and grain, or worshiping before fire altars. The masculine gender, it appears, performed in both the public sphere and the art. Moreover, this gender-based differentiation in material contexts was by no means limited to art and inscriptions. The Persepolis Fortification Tablets indicate that women and girls were sometimes allocated lesser food rations than men and boys for equal work. Also, special rations distributed to the mothers of newborn boys were greater than those provided for the mothers of newborn girls—again reinforcing the gender-based, religiously-sanctioned, social hierarchy (PF 999, 1221, 1232; see also Lewis 1990: 1–3; and Wiesehöfer 1996: 88).

There is a similar paucity of data, textual and archeological, on socioreligious aspects of Zoroastrian women's lives for over five hundred and fifty years between the fall of the Achaemenian empire and the end of the Parthian or Arsacid regime. That enigmatic time covers the period of Greco-Macedonian rule (ca. 331–312 B.C.E.), the Seleucid and Parthian kingdoms, plus the southwest Iranian state of Elymais (ca. 162 B.C.E.–224 C.E.) and the southern Mesopotamian state of Characene or Mesene (Meshan) (ca. 125 B.C.E.–224 C.E.). The Indo-Greek states of Central Asia (ca. 250–50 B.C.E.), whose populations followed many aspects of Iranian culture, also fall within that poorly known era.

After the conquest of Iran by Alexander the Great (356–323 B.C.E.), intermarriage occurred between Greco-Macedonian military officers and Iranian noblewomen (Arrian VII: IV, 4–8; Plutarch, Life of Alexander, 70). Such unions included Alexander himself taking local brides, such as Persian princesses who were daughters of Artaxerxes or Artaxshassa III Ochus (ruled 359–338 B.C.E.) and Darius or Darayavahush III Codomannus (ruled 336–330 B.C.E.) and even a Bactrian princess named Roxane or Roxana. The marriages seem to have been presided over by magi, thus possibly being conducted according to Iranian rites (see further Boyce and Grenet 1991: 11). It is unclear—and much debated—whether these events were part of a concerted effort to interlink the two cultures but, even if not, Alexander's conquest of Iran initiated the beginning of several centuries of socioreligious commonality between east and west, which transformed Zoroastrianism and its practitioners through the introduction of new divinities, ceremonies, and mores. The marriages also cemented alliances and provided political legitimacy by linking the newcomers to Iranian nobility (compare Brosius 1996: 76–79). Hence, later, Seleucus I (ruled ca. 312–281 B.C.E.) married Bactrian, probably Zoroastrian, noblewomen such as Apama (Justi 1895: 19; Frye 1984: 179; Shahbazi 1987; Boyce and Grenet 1991: 23–24)—again uniting Greek and Iranian socioreligious praxes and political lineages.[4]

The period from the middle of Achaemenian times through Greco-Macedonian and Seleucid rule also witnessed an augmentation of positive feminine roles at a spiritual level through the images of Aphrodite, Artemis or Diana, the maternal Nana or Nanaia, and others becoming Iranized—especially in connection with Anahita.[5] Hera came to be equated in worship with Spenta Armaiti (Boyce 1982: 220). Female devotees at sites even as far from the Iranian plateau as Sardis sought the favor of conglomerate divine spirits such as Artemis-Anaitis (Anahita) with whom they shared the same gender (compare Boyce and Grenet 1991: 244). A concomitant rise in the status of women occurred. Thus, women gradually came to be depicted more frequently in the official art (see Boyce and Grenet

1991: 117). It even appears that women were permitted, at least from near the end of Achaemenian times onward, to study Mazdean religious texts. Their doctrinal knowledge was credited with helping restore belief after the turbulence resulting from Alexander's conquest: "There was a nask [division of the Avesta], a nask called Bag, which had been memorized by women and a child. In that manner, the religion returned to Sistan" (Pahlavi Texts 26: 15; see further Bailey 1971: 161; Boyce and Grenet 1991: 16). Women began to function as priestesses, especially for Artemis-Anaitis in Anatolia (Boyce and Grenet 1991: 243). But, in more traditional Zoroastrian settings on the Iranian plateau their activities seem to have been limited to non-liturgical functions.

During the subsequent Parthian era, theophoric names became common for women (Colledge 1986: 5). In addition, a former slave girl made queen, named Musa (later also known as Thermusa) who most likely was non-Zoroastrian, served as co-ruler together with her son Phraataces or Phraates V (ruled ca. 2 B.C.E.–4 C.E.) whom she married. She even claimed divine status as Thea Urania in Anatolia, perhaps equated to Anahita on the Iranian plateau (Unvala 1925: 33–34; Frye 1984: 237). Other Parthian princesses are attested in the historical record, such as Rhodogune the daughter of Mithradata or Mithradates I (ruled ca. 171–138 B.C.E.) but not in connection with religious matters (see further Unvala 1925: 33). Noblewomen also were mentioned by name in contracts, pertaining to the sale of vineyards and dating from the first century B.C.E. to the first century C.E., recorded in the Greek language and in the Parthian language at Avroman in Kurdistan (see Minns 1915: 28–30). Yet, access to the harems in which these elite women and concubines dwelt may have been restricted to kings, princes, eunuchs, and female servants; and the women inside harems might have had only indirect contact with other people on the outside (see further Balcer 1993: 273–285). Issues of purity and pollution would have been combined with those of status and sexuality in the creation of those restrictions. The biblical Book of Esther (1: 10, 15, 2: 2–4, 8–17, 4: 4–6, 9–10, 7: 1–10), probably set in the Seleucid or Parthian period, offers a glimpse into the harems and activities of women in royal settings (see also Shaked 1982; J. R. Russell 1990a; for Judeo-Persian renditions consult

Moreen 2000: 28–29; 90–104, 112–116, 210–215). When traveling, granting audiences, and engaging in commercial transactions, it is likely that these women were required to maintain appropriate protocols in their dealings with men not related or indentured to their families or them.

Images of Parthian noblewomen reclining on couches are present on rock reliefs, while sanctuary and funerary statuary from locales like Hatra reveal images combining piety with opulence (Colledge1977: 86). Wall compositions of painted clay at Khaltchayan, rendered between the middle first century B.C.E. and the middle first century C.E., depict noblemen, noblewomen, and a charioteer female divinity (Colledge 1977: 95, and figures 40a–b). Clearly, religious issues of purity and pollution were no longer major impediments to women attaining positions of authority or playing public roles—especially when aided by birthrights such as rank and wealth. Their enhanced civic image was reflected in the arts and literature (see for example Kawami 1987: plates 10, 63, 64, 69; Khaleghi-Motlagh 1989: 732; Mathiesen 1992: I, 27, 32–33, 35, 37–38, 57).

At the religious level, veneration of non-Iranian, often Greek, Mesopotamian, Arabian, and Anatolian female divinities occurred. That practice is attested by images of Nike, "Victory," and Tyche, "Fortune," on the imperial coinage and by depictions of women and men in religious processions honoring Allat, "the goddess," and Cybele, an earth and mother divinity (see further Unvala 1925: 7–8; Colledge 1986: 6–8, 20–25; Choksy 1990: 202, and figure 2). Tyche also was worshipped with Zeus-Oromasdes (Ahura Mazda), Apollo-Mithra-Helios, and other Zoroastrian divinities by men and women at Commagene in Anatolia during the first century B.C.E. (Colledge 1977: plates 4, 9a). On the Iranian plateau and in Armenia, Anahita—augmented by attributes of other feminine divine beings such as Artemis and Nana—became the focus of an extensive temple cult with statuary and votive offerings (Unvala 1925: 20–21; Colledge 1986: 4–5; J. R. Russell 1987: 94, 240, 246; Boyce and Grenet 1991: 37–38, 107–108). Honoring Artemis in conjunction with Anaitis and Mah, the "Moon" divinity, became popular (Unvala 1925: 18–19). Hierodouleia or sacred prostitution by Armenian noblewomen was, allegedly, associated with some of these temple cults.[6] A more verifiable, public, religious role for women during Parthian times was as mourners in funerary settings (Colledge 1986: 25).

Unlike the meager evidence available from earlier, a much clearer picture of women's lives and roles in the interplay between feminine and masculine within religious and religiously-influenced social settings is available from the period of the Sasanian dynasty onward. Not surprisingly, again, it is the actions of elite women that are clearest in later records—for their lives often served as models of socioreligiously acceptable or unacceptable behaviors. The pious memory of Denag, as a sister, wife, *banbishnan banbishn* or "queen of queens" of Ardashir I (ruled 224–240 C.E.) who founded the Sasanian dynasty, and mother of the second king of kings Shapur I (ruled 240–272 C.E.) was commemorated in Shapur's trilingual (Pahlavi, Parthian, and Greek) inscription on a building called the Ka'ba-e Zardosht at the site of Naqsh-e Rostam in Fars province (29). Her name, title, and image were also preserved on an amethyst seal (Borisov and Lukonin 1963: 48; Harper and Meyers 1981: 34–35; Choksy 1989b: 122; Gignoux 1996: 282). Shapurduxtag I, daughter of Shapur the prince of Mesene and later queen of queens of the Sasanian king of kings Wahram II (ruled 276–293 C.E.), was commemorated for similar familial duties on Shapur I's inscription (21). Her stylized image was reproduced, alongside that of Wahram II, on the obverses of the imperial coinage (see figure 1). On those silver coins, she was shown wearing boar-headed and horse-headed bonnets symbolically associating her with the Zoroastrian masculine divinity of victory Verethraghna or Wahram after whom her husband was named (see further Choksy 1989b: 122–124, with plate 10, figures 1, 3, 5–7). She also was depicted on rock sculptures at the sites of Barm-e Dilak and Sar Mashhad in Fars province—where her husband, the king, was shown protecting his family from a lion's attack (Vanden Berghe 1959: plates 73b, 74a). Shapurduxtag II, whose noble lineage among the Sakas or Scythians helped legitimize the kingship of Narseh (ruled 293–302 C.E.), was presented jointly wielding a beribboned diadem—symbolizing sovereignty—with her husband on a rock relief at Naqsh-e Rostam (Vanden Berghe 1959: plates 30b–c; Shahbazi 1983: 265–268). The mother of prince Shapur II (ruled 309–

FIGURE 8. SASANIAN SILVER COIN IMAGE OF BORAN. Early seventh century C.E. *Courtesy of the American Numismatic Society, New York.*

379 C.E.) acted as regent on behalf of her son for over sixteen years (Agathias IV: 26; Tabari I, 836).

Documentary and numismatic evidence help reconstruct an outline of the life of the Zoroastrian queen of queens Boran who actually reigned toward the dynasty's end (ruled 629–630 C.E.) (figure 8). Royal tradition ensured that her legacy survived, together with that of her sister Azarmigduxt or Azarmeduxt (ruled 630 C.E.), as an upholder of the tenets stipulated by Zoroastrianism (see further Göbl 1971: 54, plate 15; Frye 1984: 337; Gignoux 1989; Chaumont 1990). For instance, Boran and Azarmeduxt were believed to have assumed the throne to ensure the continuity of the Mazda-worshipping royal dynasty in the absence of any male royal heirs. Thus, under specific circumstances, women's gaining absolute authority within a system that saw politics and religion as conjoined was endorsed even by magi (see further Choksy 1988b: 36–40).

The life story of Shirin, a Christian queen of Xusro II (ruled 591–628 C.E.), combining fact and fiction, was recorded in a range of textual sources including ones written in the Syriac and New Persian languages (compare Nöldeke 1883: 28; Guidi 1903: 17; Palmer 1993: 117). Involvement in sectarian politics, coupled with popular romantic notions, kept her memory extant. There also are accounts of a purported marriage between the same Sasanian ruler and Maria, a daughter of the Byzantine emperor Maurice. The alliance created by that marriage, if it indeed occurred, supposedly provided Xusro with Byzantine military support to successfully regain the throne from which, in the opinion of late Mazdean sources, he had been wrongly ousted. Once taken into the royal or princely courts, however, even the lives of non-Zoroastrian elite women such as Shirin and Maria would have changed. They must have been expected to follow Mazdean guidelines—from purity notions to spousal behaviors, modeled on those attributed to divinities like Aredwi Sura Anahita and Spenta Armaiti—and to unfailingly abjure actions which the faith regarded as negative and chaotic, even when they were permitted to retain their original confessional affiliations.

Additional observations can be made on two important aspects of elite Sasanian women's lives. Firstly, it is not clear whether women of imperial households had to veil themselves from public view when venturing outside, though it may have occurred to separate them from the gazes of commoners (Parsay, Ahi, and Taleqani 1977: 124–154). They were not shown veiled in the art of the times—although neither was their sensuality highlighted as was the case for generic representations of the feminine on luxury objects. In contrast to the seminude or nude images of nondescript women, the stylistic conventions on elite women usually show them wearing flowing robes (Harper and Meyers 1981: 32–35, and figure 9). However, numismatic evidence indicates that Sasanian kings wore a veil which draped down from their crowns—so as to separate themselves from, and to denote their superiority over, commoners while ensuring continued maintenance of ritual purity.[7] Overall, veiling does not seem to have been commonplace in ancient Iranian society. Zoroastrianism never placed such a restriction on either women or men, and the Parsis have not practiced veiling of women. Therefore, this practice may very well have been confined to the ruling class of Iran in late antiquity and the early Middle Ages—until the arrival and spread of Islam, when use of the *chador*, "scarf," began among Zoroastrian women who remained in Iran (J. R. Russell 1990b). Secondly, like their counterparts in Achaemenian times, Parthian and Sasanian royal women seem to have been granted exception to certain widespread religious praxes. Such a woman's corpse could be placed in an *aspanur* (*haspanwar*), "tomb," rather than be exposed (Karnamag i Ardashir Papakan 14: 17; compare Pahlavi Texts 55: 1–5, where the reference is to king Xusro I; see Shaki 1988: 93–95).

Other women became well-known because their actions violated established social guidelines. Christian writings highlight the newfound convictions of women who refused to follow entrenched Iranian mores. They opted for celibacy, symbolized by Mary the mother of Jesus, rather than marriage and procreation, symbolized by Spenta Armaiti and Aredwi Sura Anahita, as a sign of rejecting the religion of Ahura Mazda. Hagiography transformed these women into archetypes for other converts to Christianity from medieval Zoroastrian society to emulate. For example, the martyrology of a woman named Anahid (d. ca. 446 C.E.), a Zoroastrian convert to Christianity, at the hands of the magi has been preserved (Brock and Harvey 1987: 82–99). But for Zoroastrians, such persons were heretics considered unworthy of imitation. While conversion away from Zoroastrianism did not necessarily free women from many of the gender stereotypes, it did alter their ritual praxis so that the purity codes relating to sex, menstruation, and childbirth were much less arduous. Moreover, they would no longer be compared with a cluster of female spirits ranging from the venerated Spenta Armaiti and Aredwi Sura Anahita to the feared Drug and Jahika. The image of Mashyane could not be avoided by female apostates from Zoroastrianism, however, for it was replaced by the closely parallel one of Eve or Hawwah and contrasted with that of Mary.

Such identifiable women were the exception rather than the rule—the vast majority remained nameless. Nameless they usually may have been, but faceless they were not. During the Sasanian era, women were frequently depicted in royal, religious, and popular art—including metalwork, sculpture, seals, pottery, and painting—as wives, mothers, companions, palace workers, dancers, musicians, and others (see for example Harper 1978: figures 2a, 12, 18, 23, 25, 26, 42, 69, 70, 83, 84, 87; Harper and Meyers 1981: plates 5, 7, 36). Representation in artwork seems to be one marker of tangible change in the social and religious positions of women after Achaemenian times, probably reflecting their growing importance in the daily activities of Zoroastrian society during the Middle Ages. Yet, the sensual aspect of the feminine remained important. As a result, non-elite women often were depicted either partially or completely nude—in scenes with material objects, plants, and animals—on luxury items (figure 9) (see further Grabar and others 1967: 60–67, and plates 14, 16–23, 38).

Certain general aspects of female life that were influenced by religious law in medieval times can be identified. Using a Middle Persian or Pahlavi juridical manual titled the Madayan i Hazar Dadestan, "Book of a Thousand Judgments," dating to the early seventh century C.E., it is possible to reconstruct some avenues open to Zoroastrian women of many socioeconomic backgrounds. Such documents clearly indicate that freeborn women had certain legal rights and responsibilities. They could enter into contractual agreements and commercial transactions, they had access to inheritance, they had to fulfill debts, and they were held responsible for violations of law. In legal texts, their rights and responsibilities were recorded using secular language. In religious texts a sectarian tone was used with constant comparisons to divine and demonic female spirits. Women's rights, however, were often not on par with those of men because women's legal capacity, like that of minors, was often passive rather than active. Therefore their public actions, such as trading, often would have been mediated by adult males with whom the women had statutory relationships—fathers, husbands, sons, or guardians. Female slaves, constantly present in secular settings and occasionally attached to temples, had few rights. They were considered property to be bought, sold, and exchanged. Their legal status did not change even when pregnant or after childbirth. Fetuses and children were regarded as legally belonging to a mother's master or mistress. Moreover, the value assigned to adult female slaves and their children was lower than that of male slaves. Only in very limited situations could a slave seek legal recourse, such as if she or he had received excessively cruel treatment (see further Perikhanian 1983: 634–641, 650–658, 665–679).

All women, including female workers and slaves, were expected to observe the basic tenets of Zoroastrianism in their daily lives unless they were members of another recognized community such as the Jews or the Christians. They were required to ensure that none of their actions resembled those supposedly emanating from Drug, Daiwi, Pairimaiti, Taromaiti, Bushyasta, Jahika, Azi, Xnathaiti, and

FIGURE 9. SASANIAN SILVER-GILT EWER WITH FEMALE IMAGES. Sixth or seventh century C.E. *Courtesy of the Metropolitan Museum of Art, New York (Mr. and Mrs. C. Douglas Dillon Gift and Rogers Fund 67.10).*

Uta—i.e., no lies, deceit, denial, contempt, procrastination, lust, concupiscence, lewdness, and loquacity. Nor were women—whether freeborn or enslaved—permitted to engage in sorcery. Witchcraft was illegal, and its practitioners condemned and punished as cohorts of the Pairikas.

Marriage was a central aspect of the social role incumbent on Zoroastrian women during the Middle Ages. Divorce was discouraged as fragmenting the family unit that had come to be regarded as vital for the procreation and raising of Mazdean children. Religious and legal stipulations circumscribed marriage and divorce (see also Katrak 1965; Shaki 1971, 1999; Choksy 1989a: 88, 90–91). Each woman's consent had to be obtained before marriage. A marriage contract protected her legal and financial rights. For instance, it could be specified therein that assets brought by the bride at the time of marriage had to be returned to her if the marriage was dissolved (see further MacKenzie and Perikhanian 1969; Hjerrild 1988; Wiesehöfer 1996: 181–182). Depending upon her own social status at the time of marriage, a Zoroastrian wife could be either a *padixshay* "lawful, main, wife" or a *chagar* "dependent, levirate, wife." A woman could also enter into marriage without the consent of her male guardians, in which case she was regarded as a *xwasray* "self-sufficient wife, self-dependent wife." In certain situations legally valid unions could arise between members of the same family. For instance, a woman whose deceased father or brother had no *padixshay* wife nor a son could become *ayoken* or gain all rights as though she had been the dead man's main wife (Madayan i Hazar Dadestan I, 21–34, 36, 41, II, 4–5; see also Perikhanian 1970: 349–353; Hjerrild Carlsen 1984: 105; Shaki 1989, 1990). All four types of marriage persisted after the Arab Muslim conquest, as attested by a learned magus named Emed i Ashawahishtan (lived late ninth or early tenth century C.E.) in his Rivayat, "treatise" (24–30, 161–162). Through marriage, women were believed to fulfill the positive roles of Mashyana and emulate the spiritual virtue of Spenta Armaiti (symbolically united with Ahura Mazda, as already discussed in chapter three). Aredwi Sura Anahita was also thought to aid such women in satisfying their socioreligiously ordained maternal duties through childbirth.

Mazdean society of medieval Iran came to be known for the practice of *xwedodah*, "consanguineous marriage, incest." Although references to the significance of consanguineous marriage are numerous in the writings of late Sasanian and early post-Sasanian magi, and rote denunciations of the practice occur sporadically in Muslim sources, there is very little nonsectarian evidence for its popularity in Iran. As briefly mentioned earlier, it appears to have spread among the Achaemenian ruling family—in particular after Cambyses II married his sisters Artystone, Atossa, and Roxane—who may have picked up the practice from the Elamites as a means of consolidating power. As a royal custom it is clearly attested in the Parthian and Sasanian periods. The whims of kings, however, are only infrequently an accurate indicator of popular or prevailing custom. There is limited indication that consanguineous marriage was adopted by Iranian commoners as a legal means (the *ayoken* type has been noted above) of retaining assets within familial units. This became especially important when families faced the possibility of members leaving the Zoroastrian community and taking economic resources with them to the socioreligious group they had newly joined. But, unlike in Roman Egypt where census records indicate consanguinity was fairly widespread among the populace, there is no evidence it ever became a popular form of consummated marriage in Iran under Zoroastrian or Muslim rule—despite certain magi even giving *xwedodah* the status of a religious duty. Marriage between cousins, even first cousins, on the other hand, appears to have been popular—a practice still common among both Iranian and Indian Zoroastrians.[8]

Other details emerge with regard to the religious roles of Iranian women prior to the advent of Islam. Zoroastrian ritual manuals from that time stress the constraints regularly placed on women's activities owing to that community's fear of impurity thought to result from bleeding during menstruation and childbirth (Choksy 1989a: 94–102). So a woman could worship at fire temples, perform basic rites at the sacred fires when men were unavailable or "at her own [fire]," and on occasion gain religious learning and general literacy by attending theological colleges "except when she is menstruating" according to the Herbedestan, "Priestly Code, Religious Studies," compiled during the ninth century C.E. (5: 1–3), and the Nerangestan (I, 22: 2, 5). But they could not enroll in the priesthood owing to their being periodically regarded as polluted. Since Zoroastrians comprised the demographically and politically dominant group at many times and places in medieval Iran, their customs found widespread acceptance. Beyond the control of the magian hierarchy, however, ideas of individual worth, spiritual equality, and open access to religious institutions, coupled with resistance to the Sasanian dynasty's religiously-based social order, initially enabled Christian women—including Zoroastrian apostates who adopted the teachings of Jesus—to participate extensively within their own community as the partners of men. The fifth-century C.E., however, witnessed a subversion of concepts of gender equality within the Christian churches of Sasanian Iran. As patriarchal notions reasserted dominance, formerly Zoroastrian, now Christian women were relegated to secondary positions under male supervision—roles that emphasized virginity, chastity, penitence, and monasticism.

Overall, relationships between the genders in Iranian society during the Sasanian era were highly complex. Some roles were open to both men and women. Other roles came to be divided up into masculine and feminine ones. Generally, women were expected to accept domesticity as daughters, wives, and mothers rather than to seek public recognition, secular authority, or clerical positions. Even within the private domain of a household, only limited authority may have been available to women for determining the upbringing and the day-to-day activities of children (Perikhanian 1983: 641–646). The extent of women's actual control over the domestic sphere remains hazy because historical records granted little importance to such activities, considering these part of a biological purpose believed to have been assigned to women by god as claimed through the scriptures and exegeses of medieval Zoroastrians.

During the seventh and eighth centuries C.E., Arab Muslims succeeded in annexing lands of the Sasanian empire from west of the midcourse of the Euphrates river all the way to the banks of the Oxus river or Amu Darya and the Indus river. In cultural terms, the Iranian world of that time clearly reached even further—westward close to the Black Sea, northward into Armenia, eastward to Uzbekistan and Kazakhstan, and southward along the coastline of the Arabian peninsula. Successful military incursions by male Arab troops led to considerable disruption in the lives of Zoroastrian men and women for more than one hundred years. For some, the Arabs may have been only a fleeting experience—armies that passed by on the way to capturing additional provinces and cities. Others, however, particularly women and girls living at important urban centers, occasionally faced spending years if not the rest of their lives providing involuntary service to triumphant Muslim soldiers. Even those involuntary actions violated Mazdean customs, and were condemned by the magi as spreading the mores of Jahika. Yet other persons, while retaining their freedom, lost their social or financial standing. All this occurred despite an attitude among the Arab elite, later enshrined in the form of a pragmatic edict attributed to the caliph 'Umar (ruled 634–644 C.E.), that "maintaining the original status of Iranians" was preferable to fanning the natives' antagonism by further disrupting prevailing socioeconomic conditions as noted by al-Baladhuri (d. 892 C.E.) in the ninth century C.E. (266–267) and al-Tabari (d. 923 C.E.) a few decades later (Ta'rikh I, 2467).

Several examples can be cited with regard to the loss of personal freedom by Zoroastrian women at the time of the Arab conquest. For instance, when the town of Jalula', situated in the Diyala river basin on the border between the lowlands of Iraq and the Iranian plateau, was captured in 637 C.E., many women there "were taken as concubines and [later] bore their Muslim masters' offspring" (Tabari, Ta'rikh I, 2464). During the bitter struggle for control of Istakhr, provincial capital of Fars and a Zoroastrian stronghold whence the Sasanian royal family hailed, several noblewomen were killed, and other women from all walks of life were forced into concubinage by Arab Muslim soldiers between 644 and 650 C.E. (Baladhuri 389–390). When Muslim troops temporarily subdued the Transoxanian mercantile city of Baykand or Paykand in 674 C.E., Iranians from both genders experienced slavery. Those female residents of Baykand who retained their freedom lost it briefly to Muslim warriors during an uprising in 706 C.E., until ransomed back by their menfolk according to the local historian al-Narshakhi (d. 959 C.E.) in his Tarikh-i Bukhara, "History of Bukhara," (61–62). At Gurgan city, along the eastern Caspian shore, persistent rebellions against Arab rule ended only after Muslim commanders hanged the male

Zoroastrian rebels and led the latter individuals' women and children away as captives around the year 716 C.E. according to Ebn Esfandiyar (lived thirteenth century C.E.) in his Tarikh-e Tabarestan, "History of Tabaristan," (162–164). Nor did peaceful capitulation alter the fate of women, as at the Khurasanian oasis town of Sarakhs where residents negotiated a treaty with Muslim forces in 652 C.E. Here, and at other places further to the west, terms of surrender usually provided security only for Iranian men (Tabari, Ta'rikh I, 2887). Again, women found themselves losing their liberty—becoming concubines and servants to the newcomers, involuntary conditions that nevertheless violated their religious purity and often led to their being regarded as irreligious by Zoroastrian men. The necessity for concubines and servant women appears to have declined only after the wives of Arab soldiers joined their men stationed in the newly conquered regions (Baladhuri 413).

Wealthy Iranian women who had acquired their assets through inheritance, marriage, or commerce, like men in similar circumstances, periodically had their homes and lands confiscated by Arab commanders. Events at Bukhara are a case in point. The Sogdian residents of that Central Asian oasis settlement, led by a khatun or female leader who was serving as regent for her young son, agreed to and then broke treaties with Arab Muslims. After the city was finally captured in 709 C.E., the Arab commander had residents hand over half their property to the victors who then settled there (Narshakhi 42–43, 52–53; Tabari, Ta'rikh II, 169–170, 1201–1202). Conversion to Islam enabled some women to retain their assets—despite the general trend until 'Abbasid times not to grant any exemption from seizure of assets. The collapse of the Sasanian empire also had stripped elite women of their official ranks and the security inherent therein. Yet, beyond the nascent Muslim society's bounds, upper-class Zoroastrian males and females still found their positions respected—unless they adopted Islam in which case they were derided—by a majority of the population who remained Zoroastrian by confession until after the tenth century C.E.

It is now known that only a small fraction of Iranians chose, voluntarily or under duress, to practice Islam during the seventh century C.E. Most Mazdean men and women, usually as urban units, agreed to pay the Arab Muslims tribute in the form of a poll tax or *jizya* rather than give up their beliefs. Records suggest that, following a similar Sasanian impost called the *gazidag*, in the early decades of Arab rule no differentiation was made between men and women when it came to levying the *jizya*. So, initially, the poll tax may have been charged from the entire population of a locality, even though in later Islamic administrative praxis it came to be due only from adult males. What is clear about the early period of Muslim rule in Iran is that collection of the poll tax was left to local, non-Muslim, Iranian authorities—often those very same individuals who had gathered the *gazidag* for the Sasanians—to implement. A few examples may be cited from the plethora available. At the western city of Nihavand, a herbed or Zoroastrian theologian paid the poll tax using funds at the disposal of a local fire temple. Residents of Ray negotiated tribute payable "on condition their fire temples would not be destroyed nor anyone among them slain" (Baladhuri 318). The margrave of Merv al-Rud in eastern Iran collected the poll tax for the Arabs rather than allow any Iranians to become Muslim. Zoroastrian and Buddhist elites at Balkh did the same on behalf of all residents there (Tabari, Ta'rikh I, 2627, 2633, 2898, 2903).

Resistance to Islam notwithstanding, much of Iran's population gradually converted to Islam between the eighth and the thirteenth centuries C.E. At first, confessional change was mainly an urban phenomenon. Then, as time went by, new converts and itinerant preachers brought Muslim beliefs and customs to villagers.[9] Gender-related reasons for confessional change can be elucidated from the extant literature, although many conversions seem to have been gender-nonspecific. In one set of cases, wealthy women among the residents of locales like Takrit along the Tigris River's west bank, Qazvin in Media or Jibal, and Isfahan chose to profess the victors' faith. By doing so, they sought to retain socioeconomic and sectarian clout—rather than dissipate it through taxation and confiscation (Baladhuri 314; Tabari, Ta'rikh I, 2477, 2478).

Sex and intermarriage between Arab Muslim men and Iranian Zoroastrian women became an important, if indirect, gender-related path to Islam. After marriage, a woman was regarded by all the religious communities as having de facto accepted the faith of her new husband. Certain cross-communal unions became especially noteworthy for medieval writers. The third Shi'ite *imam* or spiritual leader Husayn b. 'Ali (d. 680 C.E.) supposedly wed Shahrbanu (d. 680 C.E.), a Zoroastrian daughter of the last Sasanian king Yazdagird III. Their son, 'Ali b. Husayn (d. 712 C.E.), became the fourth spiritual leader of the Shi'ite Muslims. This reputed convergence of Muslim prophetic lineage with Zoroastrian imperial genealogy would have associated early Islam, particularly its emerging Shi'ite version, with the cultural identity of those among the conquered who had hitherto regarded the Arabs' faith as an alien one. A similar marriage across Arab Muslim and Iranian Mazdean ethnoreligious lines occurred between the Umayyad caliph al-Walid I (ruled 705–715 C.E.) and Shahfarand (Shah i Afrid), daughter of a Sasanian prince named Peroz. Their son, in whose personage Iranian and Arabian royal lines were united, eventually reigned as Yazid II (ruled 720–724 C.E.). These women, and others like them who entered the caliphal courts, would have transmitted Zoroastrian customs such as Nav Ruz or the new year's celebration at the Spring equinox and the feast of Mithra or Mihragan at the Autumnal equinox to their Muslim spouses and made such praxis normative within Iranian Muslim society.

Following in the footsteps of Shahrbanu and Shahfarand, nondescript Zoroastrian women frequently found husbands among Arab Muslim settlers or among Iranian men who had adopted Islam. The magi tried desperately to halt this practice by condemning it as a grievous sin—irrespective of whether it occurred between a Zoroastrian woman and Muslim man or vice versa. Moreover, Muslim intellectuals, principally jurists, often took a parallel view ruling such unions invalid if the woman remained a Zoroastrian. Authorities of the Jewish gaonate, from the middle of the seventh century C.E. onward, also sought to discourage sexual contacts and weddings with Muslims by taking the position that such interactions with "[persons] in a state of impurity" would lead to the Jews involved becoming unclean too. Christians in medieval Iranian society too attempted discouraging such sexual behavior by forbidding it and by assigning to unwed women the role of nuns who cared for orphans and waifs, despite Christian women who entered Muslim households not having, in theory, to abjure their doctrines and rituals. But orthodox elites had little success in halting sexual intercourse and matrimony between non-Muslim women and Muslim men, especially as intermarriage among Zoroastrians, Jews, and Christians had occurred sporadically prior to the Arab conquest.[10] In addition, the Muslim community required that male nonbelievers who wed Muslim women convert to Islam.

Another gender-specific reason for seeking entry into the Muslim community lay in circumstances ultimately beyond women's control, namely their loss of socioeconomic status once male relatives converted to Islam. Essentially, the legal standing of a Zoroastrian woman fell if a husband, brother, or father became a Muslim. Since Zoroastrians formed the largest confessional group from whose ranks Muslims arose in Iranian society, it is informative to briefly consider the rulings by magi on this matter. A woman who found herself in such a situation could serve as the *chagar* wife of another Zoroastrian, not as the *padixshay* or main one. She then had only limited authority over any children she bore. She also became partially responsible for her own maintenance. Moreover, another Zoroastrian man usually had to function as her guardian in public settings. Surprisingly, the Zoroastrian community took no steps to rectify this situation or provide for the well-being of women and their children when placed in such plight. Concerns of abandonment by their men coupled with resulting decline in rank seem to have convinced some women to cast aside their Iranian religion in favor of the Arabian one, often taking their children with them (Pahlavi Rivayat of Adurfarrobay and Farrobaysrosh I, 2–3). Other groups did not follow the Mazdean model. Thus, for example, a woman's social and financial positions were not directly affected by the apostasy of other Christians—including male relatives. Indeed, Christian women often served as patrons, without oversight of male guardians, disposing their wealth as they saw fit (Palmer 1990: 167).

A third impetus for Zoroastrian women turning to Islam also arose from conditions peculiar to their sectarian community. As briefly mentioned earlier, elaborate purity codes required Zoroastrian women to segregate themselves while menstruating and for forty days after childbirth, then undergo purification rituals before re-mingling with their families. Beyond the domain of arduous rites associated with this notion of impurity—such as isolation, donning special clothes, and using particular utensils while eating—these women also faced the psychological distress of being regarded as periodically afflicted by a form of evil supposedly linked to Jahika and Mashyana. Abandoning the confessional system that imposed such values and activities for one in which simply bathing rendered women ritually free from impurity appears to have met with favor.[11] To some extent, the same may have been true for those Jewish women who chose Islam too.

Converting to Islam, either actively or passively, brought about a series of repercussions which further cut ties between women who had recently become Muslims and members of their former community. Reactions by Mazda-worshipers toward men and women who left their fold was generally hostile. It is instructive, for instance, to examine the Zoroastrian community's position on apostates. In spiritual terms, any Zoroastrian—female or male—who adopted Islam was branded a sinner whose soul was condemned and could never reach paradise. For a male apostate, this supposedly meant encountering a hideous Daena as described in chapter four. In regard to temporal matters, he or she came to be viewed as legally deceased and, therefore, bereft of rights and possessions. All property the individual possessed passed to family members remaining loyal Zoroastrians or in their absence could be seized by the community. Only when Muslims began to outnumber Zoroastrians, after the tenth century C.E., was it no longer possible for the latter to enforce this policy—then, a convert could count on Muslim coreligionists among the local authorities to safeguard his or her valuables. Hence, Zoroastrians eventually had "no option but to act in the most prudent, least dangerous, fashion by permitting a convert [to Islam] to retain personal assets" according to Emed i Ashawahishtan (Rivayat 11–12). So loss of a group's members was compounded by loss of assets. Giving up on apostates, other sects also sought to safeguard their finances. The gaonate, for instance, protected the Jewish community's finances by ruling that the inheritance of women remained valid even if overseen by executors who became apostates or by Islamic courts.

Severing of contact with the former group would have compelled converts to develop strong bonds to their newfound denomination. Through these latest ties much more than physical items were carried from one community to another. On a syncretistic note, many recent Muslims received religious instruction orally—during which process attempts were frequently not made to distinguish carefully Islamic doctrinal and ritual details from Zoroastrian ones. Since most Iranian female converts would have been functionally illiterate, there was no possibility of features specific to Islamic tradition being studied. As a result, Mazdean praxis entered Muslim devotions. Some converts placed lamps before the *mihrab*, "prayer niche," in mosques as a reconciliation of having worshiped in a fire altar's presence with their current devotions toward Mecca. Other women continued visiting Zoroastrian shrines, justifying their pilgrimages in the name of one or another Muslim saint. A feminine Muslim image, that of Fatima (d. 633 C.E.), daughter of the prophet Muhammad, functioned as a religious model for former Zoroastrian women to emulate as chaste females, obedient wives, and devoted mothers. Indeed, Fatima would eventually be given the epithet *zohar* or *zuhara*, "radiant (like the planet Venus)," a honorific previously held by the Zoroastrian female divinity Aredwi Sura Anahita, whose own name refers to chastity as discussed previously. Women must have been on the forefront of transmitting these and other innovations to their children, using both the Persian language and daily example.[12]

Separation from former coreligionists together with pressure to conform to Islamic mores resulted in many women changing their names and dress to meet with approval from other Muslims. Even popular female names such as Aban, Anahid, Armaiti, Fren(i), and Hwow(i), and compound names based on them, all of which have connections to Zoroastrian belief and legend, fell out of favor among recent converts to Islam. Conversely, those women remaining non-Muslim found their own public behavior increasingly regulated by the politically dominant Muslim community. Clothing, including styles and colors, became important visual markers of confessional allegiance and a means for isolating Zoroastrians, Jews, and Christians in public settings. The Umayyad caliph 'Umar II (ruled 717–720 C.E.) and the 'Abbasid caliph Harun al-Rashid (ruled

786–809 C.E.) both allegedly forbade Zoroastrians from wearing Iranian-style jackets and silk garments. During the first two hundred years of Islamic rule, however, few attempts would be made to enforce these ordinances. Around 850 C.E., once Muslims had become the dominant urban polity, the caliph al-Mutawakkil (ruled 847–861 C.E.) would command that non-Muslim men "don yellow hats" and non-Muslim women "who ventured into public places should do so only when covered with a yellow shawl." Yellow had been assigned as the color for dhimmi, "protected," communities because Muslims were forbidden from wearing garments tinted with saffron, source of the principal yellow dye in the Middle Ages. Yet, the enforcement of Muslim social norms as a means of Islamization was at best haphazard, with medieval geographers and historians noting that Zoroastrians—men and women—often ignored these stipulations unless forced to comply. The situation would have been complicated further by formerly Zoroastrian women influencing the garb their Muslim husbands and masters wore. Fabrics like silk, styles such as the Iranian robe and pants, and even colors like saffron yellow found favor among Muslim men owing to the influence of these women. Likewise, the choice of children's clothes fell within the domestic realm with mothers playing a role in determining whether their offspring eventually accepted or rejected dress codes established by Muslim administrators (see further Triton 1930: 123; Morony 1984: 259; Choksy 1997: 131–132).

Another circumstance where women crossing religious boundaries had to reconcile old traditions with new ones related to diet—both for themselves and their household members. The most notable change must have related to the consumption of pork, sanctioned by Zoroastrians and Christians but taboo to Muslims and Jews. Again, these women opened new culinary avenues for men with whom they lived as wives, concubines, servants, and slaves: meats other than pork, rice, and sugar became regular components of the diet of Muslims in medieval Iran. Even the mode of dining changed when the use of metal bowls, popular among Zoroastrians for purity reasons, was introduced to the Muslims. Women remaining among their ancestral ecclesiastic groups would have faced the additional challenge of maintaining old dietary norms in situations where contact with Muslims became inevitable. To them largely fell the responsibility of ensuring that food items prepared by Muslims satisfied Mazdean codes both in terms of the ingredients and the cooking utensils—for if either could be regarded as ritually unclean then the food would pollute a family that consumed it. Of course, supervising the cooking of food by Muslims—as advised by the magi in order to ensure maintenance of purity codes—brought Zoroastrian women into even more frequent contact with the bearers of Islamic values, exposing them to the veneration of Allah rather than Ahura Mazda, Aredwi Sura Anahita, Mithra, and other spirits (Morony 1984: 209, 259; Choksy 1989a: 103–104).

In legal terms the status of women did not experience any fundamental changes during the course of Islamization. As in Sasanian society, women—even Muslims if not freeborn—in the newly Islamic society found themselves sold, purchased, exchanged, bequeathed, and inherited. Wealthy Umayyad and 'Abbasid men often acquired many women to consolidate alliances and as status symbols, keeping large harems of wives and concubines, just as Sasanian nobles had once done. Transactions involving women as commodities even seem to have taken place across confessional lines—for example, the caliph 'Ali b. Abi Talib (ruled 656–661 C.E.) may have sold a Zoroastrian princess named Izdundad to the Jewish exilarch Bostanai (d. 660 C.E.) (see Morony 1984: 258–259, 320–321). Many aspects of daily life continued as before for women. Glimpses of them as ladies, merchants, mystics, artisans, midwives, vendors, bath attendants, and prostitutes emerge in addition to the socially championed roles of mothers, wives, and daughters. Legal injunctions from the Muslim and Zoroastrian communities of medieval Iranian society reflected the reality of such day-to-day activities, discussing not just marriage, divorce, and children, but also issues of commerce, property, liability, testimony, crime, and punishment—as recorded by the Muslim jurist Malik b. Anas in the late eighth century C.E. (Muwatta' 306) and the Mazdean cleric Emed i Ashawahishtan about a hundred years later (Rivayat 7–9).

It is clear that Mazdean women, although often ephemeral in the official record, participated actively in defining the culture and the history of both late Zoroastrian and early Islamic Iran. Through women's lives vital information emerges on what responses were induced by strife, why individuals switched group affiliations, how communal identities came to be defined or redefined, and which adaptations facilitated reconciliation of the past with the present (compare Scott 1988: 24–25, 27). Simultaneously, certain situations remained fairly constant. Within the parameters stipulated by law, Muslim women of the dehqan, "country gentry," class could exercise their economic might like their Zoroastrian forerunners once did. Low-rank Zoroastrian women entered Muslim households as concubines, maids, and slaves, just as social inferiors had once done in the society of Sasanian times. Among Mazda-worshipers, women continued to experience inflexible purity laws. They, therefore, went on converting to Islam to avoid the rigid rules of their religion. Others followed their menfolk who switched faiths. Yet others found the worship of Allah to be spiritually fulfilling. Confessionally and socially, the centuries immediately following the Arab Muslim conquest of Zoroastrian society proved, in sum, to be a transitional milieu where women and their children, one generation after the other, transmitted Mazdean features into the nascent Islamic community. Those traditions combined with Muslim ones to create an Irano-Islamic culture that flourished in the later Middle Ages—a society ostensibly Islamic but perpetuating many Mazdean features.

Thus, as Zoroastrians slipped into despondent resignation about the loss of their political authority through conquest and the diminishment of their demographic numbers through conversion, Muslim positions often prevailed after 1300 C.E. Yet these usually were reflections or modifications of earlier Mazdean views. So, after the tumult of political and religious reorientation had passed, the average woman in Iranian society during the late Middle Ages, when Islam was dominant, may well have found her life not very different in tone and structure—despite some enhanced stature and opportunities—from that of her female ancestors during late antiquity and the early Middle Ages when Zoroastrianism had prevailed. Between the fourteenth and seventeenth centuries C.E.—when the medieval period gave way to pre-modern times—Mazdean women's lives remained partially under constraint by masculine religious tenets, male-created images of appropriate divine spirits, and by a sectarian society dominated by men. An increasingly minority status within Iranian society during Mongol (1219–1256 C.E.), Ilkhanid (1256–1335 C.E.), and Timurid (1370–1507 C.E.) times, coupled with renewed persecution at the beginning of the Safavid period (1502–1722 C.E.), fueled an urge for self-preservation which in turn led to communal isolation (Boyce 1979: 177–182; Choksy 1997: 142–143). Within that setting, it continued to be suggested that societally-defined feminine traits such as domesticity, maternity, submissiveness, and piety were best for women—as reflections of the roles of holy female spirits who maintained religious order—and that public roles, authority, and leadership were at least inappropriate and even possibly dangerous—as reflections of the roles of evil female spirits who spread disorder.

CHAPTER SIX

Conclusion: Modernity & Change

The preceding discussions on ascriptions of demonic and deistic feminine images vis-à-vis masculine images and of female roles in contrast to male roles, within ancient and medieval societies, have shown that slow transformation took place over time in those representations and in the lives of Zoroastrian women. Projections of women and men, female and male, feminine and masculine were constructed in Mazdean society gradually over time, then recorded in literary and visual forms, like in other societies (see in general Clark 1998: 30–31). There was no greater period of change in beliefs, lifestyles, and art than during and after the eighteenth century C.E.

Drug was mentioned in a collection of New Persian treatises, the latest of which dates to 1773 C.E., but no longer in the sense of cosmic evil (Persian Revayats 1: 67, 73). Her alleged attempts to harm Zarathushtra, vividly described in medieval sources, though repeated in the Rehbar-e Din-e Jarthushti, a Parsi Gujarati catechism written in 1869 C.E. by the highpriest Erachji Meherjirana (21–22), is devoid of details. Devotees are simply advised in that treatise, "if you worship [her] you will be ruined" (104). Yet, despite having her power diminished in symbolic value, Drug remains a malevolent force in orthodox Zoroastrian imagination with the term *doruq* still meaning "lie." Likewise, the twentieth-century and twenty-first-century C.E. initiates of Ilm-e Khshnum, "Teaching of Joy," a Parsi Zoroastrian mystical movement, seek to subdue sexual desire for they hold that it arises from Drug to lead humans away from the divine (Chiniwalla 1942: 13–15; Tavaria 1971: 138). At present, most Zoroastrians continue to view Drug as an opponent of righteous individuals—a female spirit who is feared, but whose affects in the world can and should counteracted (Mistree 1982: 40, 54). Nasush, now often fused with Drug, also has endured as the ghoul of impurity, although pollution gradually came to be explained in exegesis as stagnation, decomposition, and degeneration (Persian Revayats 1: 111–112, 118–119, 124, 132, 2: 66; Rehbar-e Din-e Jarthushti 130, 171; see also Mistree 1982: 55–56).

Taromaiti, the Medieval she-devil of heresy and impiety, was last referred to fleetingly in the Persian Revayats (1: 52). Bushyasta, mentioned in passing in the Persian Revayats (1: 52, 2: 66), was represented as an adversary of the male beneficent immortal Xshathra Vairya in the Rehbar-e Din-e Jarthushti (146). By that time, however, she had become generally identified with sleep and dreams in popular Mazdean belief (Asmussen 1982: 119–120). Similarly Jahika, also noted indirectly in the Persian Revayats (1: 197), declined in popular conviction thereafter. Azi persisted as a maleficent spirit of avidity and lust until the early twentieth century C.E. (Persian Revayats 1: 52, 2: 66; Pazand Jamaspi 6: 6–7; Persian Jamaspi 6: 2; Rehbar-e Din-e Jarthushti 146). She eventually become simply the symbol of "greed" and "covetousness," as denoted for example by the word *az* in the New Persian language.[1] Mush was united with other Pairikas who, as a group, came to be viewed as ambivalent fairies capable of both good and evil (Persian Revayats 1: 67; Rehbar-e Din-e Jarthushti 179). Indeed, the New Persian term *pari* now denotes a "fairy."[2] Daiwi, Pairimaiti, Xnathaiti, and Uta were not mentioned frequently after the sixteenth century C.E., while Asrushti, Anaxshti, and Duzhyairya had been excluded from the demonic legions by the end of the Middle Ages. Even in her late Middle Persian form of Udag, Uta had begun to denote harmless chatter, representing the trend toward de-demonization of all but the most important of evil beings. Not only had the degree of symbolic importance attributed to feminine ghouls begun to attenuate, so too had the socioreligious power ascribed to such alleged spiritual forces.

Yet, while the powers attributed to supposedly negative spiritual entities were on the wane, the Persian Revayats of the early modern period retained the notion that, in general, men were righteous and women were potentially problematic: "The holy Zarathushtra asked

Ahura Mazda, 'Why is the father superior and the mother inferior?' Ahura Mazda replied, 'The father is superior because I first created a righteous man and pronounced blessings upon him ... [and because] the accursed Angra Mainyu first seduced woman from the true path'" (1: 172). These Revayats mark the terminus of such explicit coupling of the feminine with irreligiosity in theology. Mashyane's sins were not mentioned in the Rehbar-e Din-e Jarthushti and, in the twentieth century C.E., both Mashya and Mashyana have come to be regarded by Zoroastrians as equally responsible for the first sins of humanity (Mistree 1982: 37–38). Likewise, fear of females—mortal or demonic—and their menstrual blood have now come to be viewed by both men and women as superstition that should be rejected in favor of rational, specifically physiological, explanations (Dhalla 1975: 192–194). A major decline in association of women, menstruation, and bleeding during childbirth with impurity and, hence, disorder or evil began during the late nineteenth and the early twentieth centuries C.E. (Menant 1898/1994: III, 4–5; Jessawalla 1911: 127–128, 146–147; Marker 1985: I, 72).

In order to comprehend the reasons for the decline of diabology it is important to note that the Sasanians were exposed to both Hellenistic and Indian sciences. Sasanian-era scholars elaborated western and eastern concepts of astronomy, biology, physics, and physiology, for example. Those scientific ideas were, in turn, inherited by Islamic regimes that ruled Iran after the seventh century C.E. So Zoroastrians, under the Sasanians, the Caliphs, and later minor Muslim dynasties, slowly began to modify their beliefs and practices to better represent changing worldviews and social conditions. Additionally, the Parsis, whose ancestors migrated from Iran to India during the tenth century C.E., had become the major Zoroastrian community by the early modern period. As Parsis gradually ascended the social hierarchy in British India, they discarded many of their traditional beliefs and practices in favor of secular mores (see Hinnells 1978, 1996; Mistree 1990). Under western influence, many Parsis even attempted to represent Zoroastrianism as a religion of rational morals and ethics comparable to those of Protestant Christianity. They were rewarded commercially and socially for willingness to abandon ancient custom and to adopt changes in conformity with colonial practice. Their rising economic and societal influence, consequently, determined the trajectory of religious change that affected all Zoroastrians, even those in Iran. Essentially, transformation of their subaltern status into socioeconomic advantage occurred at the expense of long-held religious traditions.

The status of Zoroastrian women in India changed from one of domestic dependence to one of socioeconomic independence in part from expansion of ideological opinions and career options due to enhanced access to education (Hinnells 1978: 53–56; 1996: 81, 156, 174, 232, 234; Rose 1989: 1–2, 74–75; Luhrmann 1996: 98, 112–116). Emulation of nineteenth and twentieth century C.E. European—especially British—attitudes toward education, scientific knowledge, materialism, the limited role of religion, and the importance of women in society produced gradual changes which expunged many negative notions of the feminine from Zoroastrianism (Axelrod 1974: 239; Hinnells 1978: 58, 80; 1981: 37; Rose 1989: 74–78, 82–83).[3] The British system of education, introduced in India between 1820 and 1880 C.E., became an important factor in the secularization of Zoroastrian boys and girls (see further Hinnells 1978: 43–44, 57–59; 1996: 80–84, 232–233, 298–307). Initially, education of women occurred through tutors at home (compare Jessawalla 1911: 31–35, who seems to have been the first Parsi woman to be educated in the English language). Women's public education began seriously in 1849 C.E. at Bombay, and spread rapidly to Parsi communities in other cities and towns. By the late nineteenth century C.E., schools for Parsi Zoroastrian girls were very well-established and popular on the Indian subcontinent (compare Boyce 1979: 200; Noshirwani 1990: 23). By the early 1900s, education of women had even reached the Parsi community at the border town of Quetta (now in the province of Baluchistan in Pakistan) (Marker 1985: I, 39, 135, II, 50–51). In Sri Lanka (then Ceylon), commencing in the middle of the twentieth century C.E., Parsi women—after completing secondary education at secular schools—began enrolling at and graduating from universities (Billimoria n.d.: 35, 54, 61).

Examination of some didactic and literacy rates reveal the monumental effect of education upon Parsi women on the Indian subcontinent—especially in exposing them to western thought. By 1901

C.E., 9.61% of women were literate in the English language within the Parsi community, in comparison with 6.15% in the Christian community, 0.01% in the Hindu community, and less than 0.01% in the Muslim community. Between 1901 and 1931 C.E., literacy among Parsis—male and female—rose from 67% to 79% while literacy in the English language specifically rose from 31% to 53%. Moreover, by 1931 C.E., 73% of Mazdean women were literate in at least one language. In comparison, literacy among Christians remained constant at 51%, among Hindus it rose from 11% to 19%, and among Muslims it rose from 13% to 19% for the same period of time. As early as 1901 C.E., 0.5% of Parsi women were completing university education; over 68% do so now (see additionally Kulke 1974: 87–89; Langstaff 1987: 9–12; and Noshirwani 1990: 21–25).[4]

The effects of education on gender relations included an enhanced economic base for women as a group, changes in social roles and structures within the community as a whole, and secularization plus westernization of specific individuals (Hinnells 1978: 56–58). Rapid urbanization began in the 1900s, reaching 94% by 1961 C.E. among Parsis, compared to 27% for Muslims, 23% for Christians, and 16% for Hindus on the Indian subcontinent (Langstaff 1987: 17–20). Marriages arranged by relatives declined in frequency after the 1920s, as women exercised their enhanced ability to select their own spouses (Marker 1985: I, 127). At the same time, educated women in the community began to choose careers over marriage, family, and domesticity—close to 25% of Parsi women remained unmarried during the 1970s and 1980s C.E., and the community's birthrate declined drastically (Axelrod 1974: 91, 93, 123; Langstaff 1987: 20–22; Noshirwani 1990: 25–26). By the late twentieth century, women's expectations had begun to exceed the reality represented by potential male partners within the community—again reinforcing the trend in declining marital and reproductive rates (see also Luhrmann 1996: 132–135; 169–173). Another aspect of the changing relationship structure between the genders was evidenced immediately, when the practice of women eating meals after their male relatives waned rapidly (Menant 1898/1994: II, 316–318). Educated women began to play prominent roles in garnering resources for furthering the education, professional training, social welfare, and introduction to western medicine and science of their cohorts (Jessawalla 1911: 55–56; Marker 1985: I, 39, 135, II, 50–51; Billimoria n.d.: 26). During the early twentieth century C.E., women began to participate freely in numerous social and civic activities across gender boundaries—from drama, dancing, and western music to sports such as bicycling, swimming, and cricket. Their local mobility increased as they learned to drive automobiles (compare Menant 1898/1994: II, 322a, 324a–d, 326a, 328a, 344d; Jessawalla 1911: 166–168, 193, 199; Marker 1985: I, 72). Women began traveling as tourists within the Indian subcontinent and to other countries, especially England and France. They also began enrolling in European universities (Menant 1898/1994: II, 339; Jessawalla 1911: 268–499; Hinnells 1983: 114). Changes even occurred in the styles of Indian clothing worn by Parsi women, from modest saris and long blouses to finer saris and shorter blouses. Western-style dresses also became popular (Menant 1898/1994: II, 285–296).

Perhaps, most importantly, with access to education, the gender-specific views and opinions of women began to spread via documents written by women for other women to read. Such works began to criticize and challenge the patriarchal tradition that had dominated Zoroastrian society until that time (compare Jessawalla 1911: especially 36–39; Ramanna 1997). This is not to suggest, however, that the interlinked concepts of disorder and evil vis-à-vis order and good have been completely disconnected from gender. More precisely speaking, an attenuation rather than a rupture of such beliefs has occurred. Yet, the decline of beliefs on negative feminine images has enabled contemporary Parsi Zoroastrian women to move beyond the earlier religious stereotypes. Order and disorder, righteousness and falsehood, good and evil have come to be viewed as social phenomena rather than religious ones. In general, knowledge is no longer viewed as the domain of the masculine gender, and the feminine is no longer feared as a source of deceit, discord, lust, weakness, and imperfection.

The same process took place in Iran from the early twentieth century C.E. onward. In the late nineteenth century C.E., European travelers recorded that Zoroastrian men still played the main economic and public roles as merchants and farmers in a generally poor community. Moreover, at the time, Zoroastrian women continued to be harassed by Muslim men when they ventured into public spaces without their menfolk—even if they wore modest clothing that exposed only their faces, hands, and feet (Browne 1893/1984: 315, 405–407, 417–418, 481; Boyce 1979: 209). At the very beginning of the twentieth century C.E., Zoroastrian men in Iran still regarded all women as inferiors. Women were encouraged to act and dress unassumingly (Jackson 1906: 374, 386; Boyce 1979: 178). However, western-style education for boys and girls had also been introduced to Zoroastrians at Tehran, Yazd, and Kerman during the late nineteenth and the early twentieth centuries C.E. (Browne 1893/1984: 408; Jackson 1903: 379, 427; Boyce 1979: 218). The introduction of education, especially for women, was propelled by the Parsis who had founded an endowed Society for the Amelioration of the Conditions of the Zoroastrians in Persia in 1854 C.E. and sent a representative named Maneckji Limji Hataria to Iran to conduct the business of the Society. Among other accomplishments, such as increased educational and commercial opportunities, in 1882 C.E. this Society was also able to have the Qajar dynasty abolish both the *jizya* and several discriminatory laws that had been placed upon Zoroastrians by Muslim rulers many centuries earlier. By the 1930s C.E., several schools in the major cities of Iran provided comprehensive education for Zoroastrian girls—paralleling lessons which had already been available to boys (see Shahrokh and Writer 1994: 2–4, 18–21, 23–26).

With the advent of secular education, exposure to western science, and Parsi-inspired religious reform, there was a gradual reorientation in beliefs and praxis regarding evil and pollution. A decline in enforcement of purity rites took place, especially on women after menstruation and childbirth (Jackson 1903: 363, 374–375, 383; Boyce 1979: 210–212, 218–223). The practice of polygyny also ended during the early 1900s C.E., for the same reasons (Shahrokh and Writer 1994: 39). But not everything changed everywhere. In the village of Sharifabad outside the city of Yazd, for example, seclusion of women during menstruation continued into the early 1960s due to fears of the demoness Nasush. There, the genders also remained segregated during school education and at public gatherings. Domestic roles were still reserved for women, while public roles were the prerogative of men. Women prepared the food offerings for the religious ceremonies, but ritually partook of those items after the men, unlike the gender-nonspecific practice of the Parsis at that time (Boyce 1977: 40–41, 47–49, 58, 92–138, 199, 219–224; 1979: 180). But the influence of secularization eventually spread from urban Zoroastrians to their rural counterparts in Iran—especially as villagers relocated to cities in search of educational and career opportunities. A range of new professional occupations and social roles also became available to educated Zoroastrian men and women during the reign of Reza Shah Pahlavi and his son Mohammed Reza Shah Pahlavi between 1925 and 1979 C.E., enhancing the community's wealth and stature (Hambly 1991: 234). As among the Parsis of India, order and disorder, righteousness and falsehood, good and evil eventually came be viewed for the main part as gender-nonspecific social phenomena rather than gender-specific religious ones by the Mazdeans of Iran.

This process of religious and attitudinal change has been further accelerated by the international dispersion of Zoroastrians during the late twentieth century C.E. (Boyce 1979: 226–227). Immigration of Zoroastrians to the United States of America, Canada, England, and Australia, countries where the community's traditional infrastructure that had reinforced female subordination in India and Iran is less present, has brought about considerable socioreligious reorientation (Seventh North American Zoroastrian Congress 1990: 121–146). Enhanced contact between Zoroastrians and members of other faiths has led to an increase in the frequency of marriage across confessional communities, bringing new issues and concepts into familial settings (Writer 1994: 106–115; Palsetia 2001: 268–275, 321–330). Those notions are passed on to the children, reinforcing the trajectory of change. Overall, the general trend is toward social and religious liberalization on a range of issues including most gender-specific activities (Seventh North American Zoroastrian Congress 1990; Kelley, Friedlander, and Colby 1993: 141, 146). Intercommunality, rationalism, science, technology, and a culture of questioning, analyzing, rejecting older mores, and accepting newer ideas became an intrinsic part of the lives of men and women around the world during the twentieth century C.E. (Conrad 1999). Mazda-worshipers were no exception to that global trend, although the rate of ongoing change varies by location.

For all the reasons outlined, women now hold communally-important public positions among Parsi and Iranian Zoroastrian groups in the United States of America and in Canada—from leadership of Zoroastrian centers such as in the greater Los Angeles area by Farangis Shahrokh to editorship of newsletters such as the FEZANA Journal by Roshan Rivetna. The most influential and widely read communal magazine, published in Bombay and titled Parsiana, is also managed by a woman, Arnavaz Mama, and is largely staffed by women. Beyond specific individuals, Zoroastrian women now choose their own matrimonial partners, divorce their husbands if the marriages are not successful, often maintain custody of children after termination of a marriage, practice birth control, engage in a range of professional careers, inherit either according to civil law (or communal law in India), pray with the men, and do not segregate themselves in daily life. Only extremely orthodox women still separate themselves from others during menses or after childbirth.[5] At the same time, the feminine gender remains the predominant sustainer and transmitter of religion—75% of Mazdean women pray daily and teach their children about the faith in comparison to 60% of Mazdean men. Major changes not withstanding, however, certain ideas still persist—such as the notion that women should not attend religious rites while menstruating (Noshirwani 1990: 7, 11–15; Gould 1994: 180). Consequently, Zoroastrian women continue to play no role in the faith's clerical hierarchy which still upholds notions that relate ritual pollution to religious and cosmic disorder allegedly caused by female spirits like Jahika and Nasush (Rose 1989: 75, 82–83). Even a recent, steady, decline of the magi—especially within India—in demographic numbers, socioeconomic standing, religious education, and communal ranking has not, as yet, resulted in the induction of women into a gender-nonspecific clergy (Mistree 1990: 250–251).

As a result, women's religious leadership often has been channeled into heterodox movements—especially in India. One such group, the Mazdayasnie Monasterie (within the Ilm-e Khshnum movement), which subscribes to both mystical trends and holistic medicine, is lead in part by a woman named Meher Master-Moos. Members of this sect regard both genders as equal while alive and believe that souls are non-gendered and asexual after death. Pollution at a corporeal level and its association with Jahika and Nasush on the spiritual level also are far less important for them—rather, the attainment of spiritual insight and purity through mysticism is stressed (Langstaff 1987: 35–37; Mistree 1990: 238–240; Zoroastrian College 1990). Another more esoteric cult regards its female leader, Sri Gururani Nag Kanya or Nag Rani, "Cobra Queen," as a divine incarnation (Mistree 1990: 246). In Iranian towns, like Sharifabad, women have developed ritual variations partly under Muslim influence such as gender-specific visits to shrines and votive offerings—not all of which are condoned by the male clerics (Boyce 1977: 60, 62, 217, 233, 237, and figures 4b, 6a–b, 7b; Jamzadeh and Mills 1986: 23–25, 52–54).

In the early part of the twentieth century C.E., Peshotan Sanjana, a Zoroastrian highpriest and scholar, claimed "there was no community in which man had more unselfish sympathy with women than the Zoroastrian nation that lived in the eastern territories of Iran," adding "the Zoroastrian man of ancient Iran had become naturally capable of appreciating the different blessings god had bestowed upon him by the creation of womankind" (1932: 506). Far from such hyperbole, Mary Boyce has suggested in her pioneering studies on Zoroastrianism that "in general women have a dignified position in the Zoroastrian community, as men's partners in the common struggle against evil" (1989: 308 note 83; compare 1979: 27, 149, 207–208). In regard to the beliefs and rules that arose from dualism she states that "Zoroastrian women have suffered much under them, yet the orthodox observe them voluntarily, with both resignation and stoic pride" and "this discipline, like all the rest, was self-imposed" (1989: 308; 1977: 102). Yet, the picture which emerges from the present analysis colors Zoroastrianism in a different shade historically—one unlike the benign faith Sanjana and Boyce claim it has been toward the feminine, the female, and women. The lives of Zoroastrian men and women have been shaped, over the centuries, by the religion's interwoven and mutually reinforcing notions of the feminine's presumed spiritual, moral, and physiological deficiency, and supposed penchant for disharmonious actions. The literature was rarely self-reflective. Only during the nineteenth, twentieth, and twenty-first centuries C.E., have Zoroastrians and some non-Zoroastrians claimed that the faith was, and is, for the most part free of gender stereotypes (compare Karaka 1858: 197; Taraporewala 1937; Kulke 1974: 104; Hinnells 1981: 36–37; Dadachanji 1986: 133).

In specific situations, the feminine was perceived by the Mazdean tradition of ancient and medieval times as negative owing to its having been linked with agents of cosmic disorder. Within the framework of religious belief, the female often became the personification of socially undesirable traits. As a result, women came to be partially viewed as instruments by which evil forced men to succumb to chaos. Dualism and patriarchy combined to produce bipolarity and opposition. On a primary level, this opposition was manifest in the distinction that Zarathushtra is presumed to have invoked through devotional poetry: a duality between Ahura Mazda and Angra Mainyu, male versus male. At a secondary level, through a theology enhanced by the magi, bipolarity came to be played out as masculine against feminine: male struggling against female. Those aspects of human behavior which came to be feared and disapproved by society and religion as disruptive forces were projected, at times, on a group to which men are attracted, yet are enjoined to disavow under certain circumstances: women. Thus, some women were seen as violating restrictions imposed on them by gender-based socioreligious constructs. While female divinities do exist in Zoroastrianism, their attributes and roles are carefully circumscribed by the faith's notions of order, good, and gender. In essence, their virtue is a direct result of definitions which place them beyond the pale of evil, and protect them from any assignation of chaotic harm. Gender, thus, constantly played an important role in the shaping of Mazdean beliefs and practices from more ancient Indo-Iranian ones (contra in general Boyce 1989: 200).

The range of socioreligious, chaotic, evil imputed to the feminine by Zoroastrianism bears analogies with the seven deadly sins in Christianity.[6] Despite cultural differences, societies whose power structure was based on gender-related constructs which reinforce patriarchy have tended to view the feminine as potentially evil and to uphold the masculine as the normative, essential, order. Since the male represented the ideal, the female became not only imperfect but also a well-spring of imperfection and, by extension, could be considered wicked and demonic. As woman, the feminine is required for the bearing of the children of men and, therefore, tolerated. As demoness, the feminine came to be abjured as a symbol of disharmony and, hence, evil, who was to be neutralized through pious actions (compare Savramis 1974: 61, 64). Not surprisingly, such opinions were often integrated into society by the use of religion as a means of legitimacy, as in the case of Zoroastrianism. Negative attitudes, however, did not mean that women were excluded from the Zoroastrian cult, Iranian royal courts, or the labor force—as discussed in chapter five (see also Harper 1971: 503, 513–514; Cook 1985: 226; Hallock 1985: 594, 601–602, 608). Thus, as mentioned previously, women of the Sasanian royal family could even serve as regents, like the mother of the infant monarch Shapur II, and as rulers, like Boran followed by her sister Azarmeduxt in the waning years of the dynasty. But, for reasons of ritual purity and pollution, at no time could women serve as members of the priesthood (Weber 1956/1978: I, 605).

The question arises whether an intensification in perceptions of the feminine and the female as negative were attempts by the Mazdean hierarchy to counter a change of women's status from subservience to independence in the latter part of the ancient period or in the early years of the medieval period. Little is known about the social dynamics of the earliest community, particularly prior to the presence of Mazda-worshipers on the Iranian plateau. The only details on the status of women and the role of gender in daily life come from the Avesta itself. However, such images may be prototypical with an indeterminate historicity (see further Kellens 2000: 93). Zarathushtra is believed to have sought the assistance and influence of Hutaosa, wife of kavi Vishtaspa, in gaining acolytes (compare Yasht 9: 26, 17: 46). Mazdeans eventually came to honor the *fravashis* of notable early women presumed to have been the devotional poet's followers, including one of his wives Hvovi, his three daughters Freni, Thriti, and Pouruchista, and queen Hutaosa (Yasht 13: 139–141). This should not be surprising, for Mazda-worshipers were enjoined to praise the *fravashis* of all righteous men and women (Yasht 13: 143–145, 148–149, 154–155). Still, respect for the immortal spirits of women after death does not appear to have translated into social equality during life in ancient times. Yasna 53, perhaps a wedding sermon delivered by Zarathushtra at the marriage of Pouruchista to Jamaspa the legendary seer, states: "Indeed, I shall unite in marriage her among you, she who will serve father, husband, pastor, and family" (53: 4). Another Gathic Avestan image of feminine meekness, evoked by the devotional poet and linked to a promise of bountifulness possibly intended as a metaphorical representation of spirituality itself, is that of the Soul of the Cow (Geush Urvan)—again a passive image equated with order and goodness—which laments its suffering and pleads for rescue (Yasna 29: 1–3, 6–9, 31: 9–10, 44: 20, 48: 5–6; see also Insler 1975: 134–135, 141–143; Humbach and Ichaporia 1994: 26–29, 70–71, 84–85).

By the time extant Pahlavi codices were written, the medieval social structure had been firmly established and the texts largely reflected that system. Yet, as the Avesta and its Zand indicate, diabolical aspects attributed to the feminine do not seem to have developed in response to an increase in women's power or influence within the ancient and medieval communities. This, of course, does not exclude the possibility of such a change having taken place. It is, however, more likely that, as with medieval Christianity, Zoroastrian notions of the demonic, in contrast to the deistic, feminine were not simply a defensive reaction on the part of men but rather the product of patriarchal cultural attitudes that developed over centuries. Generally, in this process, male and female were compared, contrasted, and assigned differential valence—orderly, righteous, truthful, self-controlled, rational, and perfect as a foil for disorderly, evil, deceitful, lusty, emotional, and imperfect (compare Bynum 1986b: 257–258). The elaborate demonology that resulted, while a medieval, Sasanian aggregate, had its basis in more ancient times and eventually formed a coherent unity with many other aspects of Zoroastrianism (Asmussen 1974: 239–241).

Evidence suggests that the relative status of various Indo-Iranian spiritual beings who eventually were assimilated into Mazdean belief varied. A case in point is the rise of Ahuras such as Mazda and Mithra—and occasional, fleeting, mention of their female counterpart, the water spirit named Ahurani—to the ranks of divinities and the decline of Daevas to the status of demons in Mazdaism (Schlerath 1985b: 688; Bishop 1987; Boyce 1989: 23–24, 52–53, 83–85). The converse occurred to Asuras and Devas in the Vedic tradition of India. As a corollary, could the demonesses of the Zoroastrian tradition have been Indo-Iranian deities who were demonized in order to discredit their praise in devotional poetry, eliminate their inclusion in rites of worship, and minimize their depiction in communal art? Once again, no details survive to suggest that such was the case. These demonesses first appeared on the scene in the early stages of Mazdean doctrinal evolution and their transition was not from good to evil, but, at the most, from innocuous to harmful before losing their dark side or fading away from modern thought.

The secondary status allocated to women was also reflected in the medieval terminology relating to sex and gender. The Pahlavi terms for "woman," *zan* and *narig*, are both synonymous with "wife." *Narig* also means "female," equating the female with woman and wife, and is based on the term for "man" and "male," *nar*. The abstract nouns for "feminine" and "femininity," *madagag* and *madagih* respectively, are based on the adjective for "female," *madag*, which is derived from the word (noun) for "mother," *mad*. Hence, in language as in society, the feminine and the female were linked with wifehood and motherhood by the Middle Ages. This is not the case for the terms that denote "man," *mard* and *nar*, neither of which bear any association with marital status. Nor are the adjectives and the abstract nouns for "male," *mardan* and *nar*, "masculine," *mardanag*, and "masculinity," *mardanagih*, connected to the term for "father," *pidar*.[7]

The theology that held the female as subordinate did not, as mentioned at the beginning of this study, permit the feminine to be the absolute locus of evil. Demonesses, like women, were regarded as the "handmaidens of the devil"—powerful through association with evil, often sinful, and periodically dangerous. But, even in this aspect they were denied absolute control and independence for their power was said to originate from the masculine evil spirit Angra Mainyu.

Nonetheless, their standing among the forces of darkness came to be regarded as loftier than their role in the legions of light. The presence of Angra Mainyu as sovereign lord of all evil did not obfuscate the hazard of feminine vice nor diminish the trials to which male devotees were supposedly exposed by female demons and dangerous women. Concepts and stories produced by the Zoroastrian clerics in late antiquity and medieval times were intended, consciously and unconsciously, to serve social functions in addition to religious ones. The past was being reconstructed to structure the present and the future (see in general McGann 1989: 106). As doctrines, exegeses, myths, and eventually artifacts, those ideas became forms of social memory that established and perpetuated specific values, ideals, and behaviors (compare Detienne 1986: 33, 38). Yet, precisely because such notions and representations served social roles, as the needs of individuals and of the collective in Zoroastrian society changed during modern times so did the communal memory relating to religious beliefs, theologies, stories, and artworks—gradually attenuating negative aspects which had previously been attributed to the feminine, female, and women.

In conclusion it should be noted again that the relevance of vivid demonology and of differential attitudes toward the feminine, female, and women—in contrast to attitudes toward the masculine, male, and men—has attenuated in the daily lives of a majority of contemporary Mazdean women and men. For many votaries, order and disorder, good and evil, gender roles and socioreligious mores have taken on more secular facets. As observed at various points in this study, such doctrinal adjustments and, consequent, wide-ranging communal transformation are largely direct consequences of western-style, non-sectarian, social and educational settings (see further Kulke 1974: 104–108; Writer 1994: 30–33, 158–159, 180–181; Maneck 1997: 182–184, 231–234). Essentially, it is clear that Zoroastrian communities reshaped their worldview recently by drawing upon new ideas and customs, including fresh approaches toward gender-related issues. As a result now in secular, urban, settings the feminine is often perceived as the dominant, vibrant force within the community with the masculine being viewed as passive—especially by women themselves (compare Luhrmann 1996: 175–179). But changes resulting from modernity notwithstanding, the feminine, female, and women still remain a source of potential danger in the minds of those orthodox individuals who conservatively adhere to the religion's older precepts—especially within traditionalist towns in the Gujarat province of India and in the Yazd region of Iran. Most importantly, as a central feature of the historical development of Mazdaism or Zoroastrian religion and of Mazdean or Zoroastrian society, the concept that the demonic feminine was more powerful than the divine feminine shaped the day-to-day lives of many Mazda-worshipers, especially women, for over three and a half millennia.

Notes

CHAPTER ONE

1. Periodization of the faith's history can also be viewed in terms of communal developments:

    Nascent communities, probably in Central Asia, with an oral poetical and eventually an oral scriptural tradition (ca. 1750–550 B.C.E.); followed by a majority religion of peoples in the Iranian empires with concomitant oral and written scriptural and exegetical traditions (ca. 550 B.C.E.–651 C.E.)—both timeframes together roughly equivalent to antiquity.
    A political minority faith in Iran and Central Asia with a written exegetical tradition (ca. 651–1300 C.E.)—a timeframe roughly equivalent to the Middle Ages.
    A political and demographic minority faith, first in Iran, then India, and recently in many countries, with a written exegetical tradition (ca. 1300–present)—a timeframe roughly equivalent to the pre-modern period plus the modern period.

2. J. P. Butler (1999), on the other hand, has suggested that there is little distinction between gender and biological sex, and that gender is not based largely on social mores but rather on normative structures from which biological gender arises. Her analysis, while possibly appropriate for other cultures, is not applicable to nor validated by developments in Zoroastrianism's religious history.
3. Additional discussions about the roles of women during

Achaemenian, Sasanian, and early Islamic times are available in studies by Brosius (1996), Frye (1998), and Rose (1998)—all concentrating on sociopolitical aspects rather than on the socioreligious facets discussed in chapter five of this book.

For more focused discussions on the socioreligious transformation of Zoroastrian women's lives during modern times see in general Boyce (1977) and Rose (1989)—both examining events within traditional settings, whereas chapter six of this book examines both traditional and changing contexts.

4. The multifaceted confluence of rituals, symbols, and beliefs within Mazdaism, where performance binds together all aspects of faith and society, has been elucidated in detail by Duchesne-Guillemin (1966: 133–156), Zaehner (1976: 119–130), and Choksy (1989a: xx–xxiv).

CHAPTER TWO

1. On the early Iranian tribal migrations see most recently studies by Hiebert and Lamberg-Karlovsky (1992), Carter (1994), Sumner (1994), and Waters (1999), who reassess archeological and/or textual evidence.
2. The social organization which may have existed among the earliest Iranians was described in detail by Geiger (1885–1886). More recently, see insightful studies by J. R. Russell (1996: 198–199, 203–204) and Windfuhr (1999: 296–316). Also eventually consult Choksy (forthcoming).
3. The many languages of Mazdean or Zoroastrian devotional poetry, scripture, exegesis, epic, and literature can be classified as:

> Old Iranian languages (ca. 1750–300 B.C.E.), specifically Avestan (which would be written, however, only in medieval times) and Old Persian.
> Middle Iranian languages (ca. 300 B.C.E.–1200 C.E.), specifically Middle Parthian, Middle Persian or Pahlavi, and Sogdian.
> New Iranian and Indian languages (ca. 800 C.E.–present), specifically Classical Persian, Modern New Persian, Parsi Old

Gujarati, and Parsi Gujarati.

For detailed analyses of linguistic developments, scripts, and conventions for the transcriptions of these Iranian and Indian languages consult Dave (1935), Gajendragadkar (1974), Schmitt (1989b), and Daniels and Bright (1996).

4. On the meaning of Ahura Mazda or Mazda Ahura see further Boyce (1985a) and Humbach (2000). On the presence of the name in Assyrian texts see Dandamayev and Lukonin (1989: 321).

On the original notion of *mainyu*, "mentality, consciousness," see Kellens (2000: 75–76, 105). The assimilation and subordination of Spenta Mainyu into Ahura Mazda in earliest Zoroastrianism is discussed by Kreyenbroek (1993: especially 101).

5. On the rise of patriarchy and its significant role in shaping societies see, in general, the insightful study by Lerner (1986: 212–229).

6. Centrality of the human element in the dualist representation of Mazdean belief has been subjected to detailed, eloquent study by Boyce (especially 1979, 1992). Her conclusions have shaped the opinions of many other scholars of Zoroastrianism, and have influenced a reinvigoration of dualism within the Parsi community through the writings of communal leaders such as Mistree (1982).

7. See further the general surveys by Jafarey (1991) and Gould (1994) plus an analysis of Zoroastrian stereotypes by de Jong (1995), all three of which should be used cautiously because their conclusions are based on limited data. Entries and references in Young (1999), unfortunately, contribute very little to analyses of the feminine, female, and women in Zoroastrianism.

CHAPTER THREE

1. A translation of the entire Fravarane is provided by Choksy (1989a: 139–140).

2. Darius I claimed that uprisings occurred when "the lie [or disorder] grew great in the land" (Behistun or Bisitun inscription 1: 34).
3. Choksy (1989a: 58, 141) describes the performance of the Kem Na Mazda prayer and provides a complete translation.
4. Additional information about, and analysis of, the twelve-thousand-year sacred and semi-mythic history is provided by Choksy (1986: 239–240; 1989a: 128–131).
5. See also the important overview by Gray (1929: 204, 212). Daiwi appears to have been fused with a male demon called Freftar, "Deceit," by the Middle Ages.
6. Many further details on these female demons and male divinities are found in studies by Gray (1929: 89–99, 106–110, 138–139, 199, 201) and Gershevitch (1967: 26–44).
7. A detailed analysis of the relationship between the Whore demoness and women, as perceived by the medieval codifiers of the Bundahishn, is provided by Choksy (1988a: 75–79). Contra Zaehner (1972: 187–191; 1976: 42–44) who did not reflect the medieval understanding precisely.
8. The notion that the devil and demonic spirits are present in or linked to women whose sexuality threatens men is fairly common. Compare the events involving the conflated images of Mary Magdalene "from whom seven demons had gone out" (Luke 8: 2), Pelagia the Harlot in fourth century C.E. Antioch who claimed she had been "Satan's evil snare" and after whose conversion to Christianity "Satan appeared ... furious, ... [and] wailed out loudly" (Brock and Harvey 1987: 49, 53), and Mary the Harlot, a woman from the village of Qidun near Edessa who lived in the fourth century C.E. and became a prostitute after Satan "assaulted her with his blandishments, bespattering her with the mud of his lust" (Brock and Harvey 1987: 30). This theme of unbridled lust continues to the present day in more secular guises, as in pornographic movies like The Devil in Miss Jones. Essays in a volume edited by Sharma (1987) provide details about the cross-cultural stereotyping of the feminine as temptation, lust, discord, and willful lack of self-control.
9. Compare the term *fravashi* which is feminine in gender, even

though there is no evidence that these immortal spirits were thought of as female. See further Bartholomae (1979: 992–995) and Malandra (1983: 103).
10. Manichaean influence on the augmentation of the Zoroastrian Azi during the Middle Ages has been analyzed well by Zaehner (1961: 223–231; 1972: 166–168, 170) and Sundermann (1978: 497–498).
11. On the range of this passage's theological and sexual implications see Choksy (1989a: 89–90). A further, important, textual survey of Spenta Armaiti is found in Gray (1929: 47–51).
12. More details are provided by Gray (1929: 55–62), Boyce (1982: 29–30, 202–204; 1988a: 277–282; 1989: 52, 71–74, 176), Malandra (1983: 117–120), Chaumont (1985: 1006–1009), and J. R. Russell (1987: 243–253).
13. Artistic depictions of specific Zoroastrian female divinities and demonesses generally are sparse. As mentioned, the most notable exception was Anahita who frequently appeared on Sasanian-era rock reliefs and coins in forms that hearken back to her Avestan anthropomorphic description as apparent in figure 1. Also consult Bier (1985: 1009–1011), Colledge (1986: 15), and Choksy (1989b: 126–133). Regarding possible earlier material images of Anahita see Boyce and Grenet (1991: 38, 234–235, 244–245).

It is important, however, not to confuse specific instances where Anahita was depicted with generic representations of female divinities or of women. One example of a generic female divine being is found on a lapis lazuli seal from Persepolis possibly dating to the Achaemenian period (Schmidt 1939: 42, and figure 25 PT4 554). General images of women from a variety of social ranks and occupations were numerous in Iranian art—especially on metalwork, in sculpture, and within manuscripts of the Zoroastrian community—on which see further chapter five of this book.

CHAPTER FOUR

1. Christensen (1917) surveyed all extant sources for the legend of Mashya and Mashyana. Zaehner (1961: 267; 1976: 70) alluded to Near Eastern prototypes.

    A ninth-century C.E. Zoroastrian named Mardanfarrox the son of Ohrmazddad provided synopses and critiques of the Judeo-Christian and Muslim myths of Adam and Eve in his Shkand Gumanig Wizar (11: 61–77, 352–358, 13: 15–41, 106–148). See also Menasce (1945: 130–133, 152–153, 182–185, 188–193) and Neusner (1986: 179–180, 183–184, 193–194). Yet, that medieval Zoroastrian scholar avoided vexing questions raised by his own exposition about the parallel tale in Zoroastrianism.

2. The biblical myth of Adam and Eve probably dates to between 1000 and 900 B.C.E. On the imagery of the Fall see also Bird (1974: 71–77) and Pagels (1988: xxi–xxii, 62–63).

    Variations in the Islamic tale of Adam, Eve, and Shaytan (Satan) or Iblis—especially within the Shi'ite tradition that developed in Iran—are discussed by Awn (1983: 40–46).

3. Having sinned, fallen from divine favor, and stripped of royal fortune, Yima could be vanquished by his adversaries, it was believed. According to the Zamyad Yasht (19: 46) "Yima [was] cleaved into two" by a brother named Spityura. By the time an account in the Bundahishn was compiled, Spityura (Spedur) had been linked with the evil Azhi Dahaka (Azdahag, Zahhak) in bifurcating Jam. Thereafter when Ferdowsi composed his Shah nama, in which the literary tussle for kingship took place between Jam (Jamshed) and Zahhak, the arch villain alone meted out such an end to the fallen hero—as depicted in a miniature painting (Zaehner 1961: figure 39). Clearly, being cut into half hearkens back to Yima's origin as the masculine twin of a primordial pair that included a feminine counterpart—and symbolically emphasizes the separation of the genders. In Vedic myth, too, Yama was tainted by evil, eventually becoming the ruler of the underworld. On Yima and Yama see further the important discussions by Lommel (1927: 196–207), Zaehner (1961: 126–127, 131–137,

139–143), Dumézil (1971), Malandra (1983: 175–178), Boyce (1989: 92–97), and Humbach (1996: 71–82).
4. In Manichaeism, however, Eve's attributes were less negative than in the Judeo-Christian tradition and she even was regarded as a source of wisdom much like her Gnostic counterpart (M 129). See Sundermann (1994).
5. Specific details on the ancient, medieval, and modern rites surrounding the disposal of corpses in Zoroastrianism are provided by Boyce (1977: 148–156; 1989: 325–330) and Choksy (1989a: 17–19, 107–110).
6. A complete account of Zoroastrian notions of the afterlife, with a careful study of the relevant texts, is available in Pavry (1929: 28–45).
7. Similarities between the ascribed images of Anahita and Daena may explain why the latter, like the former, became popular in medieval art unlike other Mazdean spiritual beings.
8. Detailed overviews of the beliefs surrounding the Daena's role in Manichaeism, and that entity's probable assimilation from and connections to medieval Zoroastrianism, are provided by Jackson (1923, 1930) and Skjærvø (1995: 277–280).

CHAPTER FIVE

1. On the issue of the religious beliefs of early Achaemenian rulers—especially the extent to which they were Mazda-worshipers and how their personal piety did or did not affect state policies toward other sectarian communities within the empire—see the slightly differing opinions of Boyce (1982: especially 41–42; 1988b), Frye (1984: 120–124, 133–134), Schwartz (1985: 684–695), and Kellens (2000: xiv, 25–26, 30), contra partially Dandamayev (1989: 347–366). Essentially, it is appropriate to suggest that Mazdean beliefs and rites had become central to Iranian religiosity with features specific to that time period.
2. An excellent study of citations about elite Achaemenian women and their relationships with men, preserved in Greek, Latin, Old Persian, and Elamite sources, is by Balcer (1993). Further primary

references to the queens and princesses mentioned in this chapter, among other noblewomen, can be found therein (Balcer 1993: specifically 49, 57–58, 61, 63, 69, 73, 77, 79–80, 86–89, 98–99, 103–104, 111, 113–114, 117–118, 131, 138, 154, 200–201, 239–240, 251, 253, and generally 279–282, 294–300).
3. Unfortunately, no indubitable funerary materials relating to Achaemenian nobility have been discovered in conjunction with human remains. There was a controversial find of a woman's corpse in Baluchistan, now a province of Pakistan. Her cadaver, wearing a golden crown similar to those of Achaemenian kings as depicted on their gold coins (known to scholars as darics), appears to have been mummified and then placed in a sarcophagus. Her body bears a breastplate claiming she was a daughter of Xerxes I. On her sarcophagus is an Old Persian cuneiform inscription which, paralleling that by Darius I at Behistun (4: 73), refers to *patikara*, "symbols, images," that should not be destroyed—such as the winged figure, possibly representing Ahura Mazda and widely-used by the Achaemenians, carved next to the text. However, this mummy is a classic example of an item not located in situ within a documentable archeological context, coupled with attempts to sell it on the global antiquities market. Examination suggests inconsistencies in the funerary inscriptions and materials. As a result, that corpse's historical authenticity is disputed (Ibrahim 2001; Romey and Rose 2001).
4. For a detailed listing of women mentioned in Seleucid documents consult Grainger (1997).
5. See in general Boyce and Grenet (1991) who amply document the complex socioreligious syncretism which arose during that time period. The fusion of Anahita with Mesopotamian and Greek female divinities has been discussed in chapter three of the present book. On Anahita's syncretistic image see also Cook (1983: 148, 150). Brosius (1998) argues for a unidirectional flow of religious influence from Iranian society to Greek society. While the case made by Brosius for the Persianization of Artemis' cult is valid in broad terms, it is not possible to accept her exclusion of Hellenistic influences on Anahita's image reaching the Iranian plateau because the resulting, fused, divinity would explain

Anahita's major symbolic role later under the Sasanians.
6. On this unresolved issue see the insightful comments by J. R. Russell (1987: 248–249), who refers to the classical sources. Marglin (1987: 309), on the other hand, merely makes the assertion that hierodouleia was connected with the worship of Anahita in temples without citing supporting evidence.
7. Evidence for the veiling of monarchs comes from *drahms* or silver coins minted by each Sasanian king of kings where the folds of a fine gauze were etched on the cape and globe of the crown. See further Göbl (1971: 7–8). This veil was lifted up, over the face, on the royal coin portraits but may have been lowered when the monarchs met with commoners. The tradition of Iranian monarchs staying out of public view is even attested by the Book of Esther (5: 1–2) which mentions the ruler seated alone enthroned, possibly behind a screen, in the inner court to which access was granted for others selectively by his consent. Additional references to the seclusion of Sasanian rulers are found in Choksy (1988b: 42).
8. The most balanced assessment of this issue to date is by Frye (1985). See also Boyce (1982: 75–77), Brosius (1996: 45–46), and Wiesehöfer (1996: 84–85). On Cambyses II's action see Herodotus (III: 31). Perikhanian (1970: 644) unfortunately overstates the case by interpreting occurrences of *xwedodah* among ruling families and its mention in magian juridical guidelines—i.e., instances limited to a few elites and to hypothetical legal situations—as definitive evidence for supposedly widespread practice. The range of possible intra-familial marriages in ancient Iran is discussed by Balcer (1993: 285–288). The data on incestuous marriages in Egyptian society has been assessed by Hopkins (1980).
9. The standard statistical study on conversion to Islam in Iran is by Bulliet (1979: 23, 43–44). Detailed information on patterns of conversion by medieval Zoroastrians to Islam is provided by Choksy (1997: 76–93).
10. Menasce (1967: 229–230) and Choksy (1987: 24), both translate and discuss the main Zoroastrian source—Emed i Ashawahishtan's Rivayat. Malik b. Anas (d. 795 C.E.) (216), Abu

Yusuf (d. 798 C.E.) (66–67, 88–89), and al-Ghazali (d. 1111 C.E) (81) are the main Islamic sources. See also Morony (1984: 238–239, 309–310). The geonic citation was a specific response by Jewish administrators concerned about the intermingling of religious communities in large cities like Baghdad (Geonica 203–204).

11. Direct reference to Muslim attempts at allaying fears surrounding menstruation among potential female converts from Zoroastrianism is found in a *hadith* or religious tradition attributed to 'A'isha bt. Abi Bakr (d. 678 C.E.), the prophet Muhammad's favorite wife, as eventually recorded by al-Sahmi (lived eleventh century C.E.) (83). On this tradition see further Bulliet (1994: 33–34).

12. Regarding the conflation of devotional trends see additional details provided by Amoretti (1975: 510–511), Frye (1975: 101, 140–141), and Bulliet (1990: 128–131).

On the assimilation of Anahita's image into that of Fatima consult the Tafsir, "commentary," on the Qur'anic passage 2: 102 by Tabari (Jami' al-bayan 485). For a partial discussion on this issue refer to Duchesne-Guillemin (1985b: 258–259).

CHAPTER SIX

1. The Jamaspi or Jamaspig is a compilation of prophecies attributed to Jamaspa the legendary seer to the kavi named Vishtaspa who may have been Zarathushtra's son (see Kellens 2000: 83–84). The text has been reworked repeatedly at different times between the ninth and the nineteenth centuries C.E., first in Iran in the Pahlavi language and then in India in the New Persian and Pazand languages.

2. Boyce (1977: 62–67) mentions the Shah Pari, "fairy queen," who is still alleged to kidnap infants in contemporary Iranian folklore. Such tales clearly reflect a continuing, ambivalent, mythic status between good and evil.

3. The general relationship between science, secular education, westernized communities, and a decline in demonology has been analyzed by J. B. Russell (1986: 128–167, 226, 297–301).

4. An excellent contemporaneous overview was recorded by Menant (1898/1994: III, 175–196). Kulke (1974: 78–91), Hinnells (1978: 42–64, 88–92), and Langstaff (1987: 4–6) provide detailed surveys of the spread of education among Parsis from 1820 to 1880 C.E. Mistree (1990: 227, 230–234), offers an excellent analysis of changes in traditional beliefs and praxes due to education.
5. Communal traditions on marriage, divorce, custody of children, inheritance, and menstruation, plus changes in these customs due to the secular influences of modernity are discussed in detail by Choksy (1989a: 89–91) and Noshirwani (1990: 16–19).
6. On the role of the seven deadly sins, particularly between the seventh and sixteenth centuries C.E., see the important study by Wenzel (1968).
7. For these terms see further Sanjana (1932: 519), Nyberg (1974: 126–127, 129, 136, 228–229), and MacKenzie (1971: 53, 54, 58, 98).

Bibliography

Complete bibliographical information for the following can be found under the name of the author, editor, or translator, or under the text's title. Multiple editions and translations are listed so that readers can refer to any one of several standard renditions.

ABU YUSUF: trans. A. Ben Shemesh.
AGATHIAS: ed. R. Keydell.
ARAMAIC RITUAL TEXTS FROM PERSEPOLIS: ed. and trans. R. A. Bowman.
ARDA WIRAZ NAMAG: ed. and trans. M. Ph. Gignoux; ed. and trans. M. Haug and H. J. Asa; ed. and trans. F. Vahman.
ARRIAN: ed. and trans. P. A. Brunt.
AVESTA (Gathas, Siroza, Videvdad, Visperad, Xwurdag Abestag, Yashts, Yasna): ed. K. F. Geldner.
BALADHURI: ed. M. J. de Goeje.
BIBLE: New Oxford Annotated Bible; Tanakh.
BUNDAHISHN: ed. T. D. Anklesaria; ed. and trans, B. T. Anklesaria; trans. M. Bahar.
CHIDAG HANDARZ I PORYOTKESHAN: ed. and trans. M. F. Kanga.
CHRONICA MINORA: ed. I. Guidi.
DADESTAN I DENIG: chaps. 1–40, ed. T. D. Anklesaria; chaps. 1–40, ed. and trans. M. Jaafari-Dehaghi; chaps. 41–92, ed. P. K. Anklesaria.
DENKARD: ed. M. J. Dresden; ed. D. M. Madan.
EBN ESFANDIYAR: ed. A. Iqbal.
FARZIYAT NAMA: ed. and trans. J. J. Modi.
GATHAS: see Avesta; ed. and trans. H. Humbach; ed. and trans. H. Humbach and P. R. Ichaporia; ed. and trans. S. Insler; ed. and trans. J. Kellens and E. Pirart.
GEONICA: ed. and trans. L. Ginzberg.

GHAZALI: trans. M. Farah.
GIZISTAG ABALISH: ed. and trans. H. F. Chacha.
HADHOXT NASK: ed. and trans. M. Haug and H. J. Asa; trans. M. F. Kanga.
HANDARZ I OSHNAR: ed. and trans. B. N. Dhabar.
HERBEDESTAN: ed. F. M. Kotwal and J. W. Boyd; ed. P. Sanjana (as Nerangestan); ed. and trans. H. Humbach and J. Elfenbein; ed. and trans. F. M. Kotwal and Ph. G. Kreyenbroek; trans. S. J. Bulsara.
HERODOTUS, History: ed. C. Hude; ed. and trans. A. D. Godley.
JAMASPI: ed. and trans. J. J. Modi.
KARNAMAG I ARDASHIR PAPAKAN: ed. and trans. E. K. Antia.
MADAYAN I HAZAR DADESTAN: pt. 1, ed. J. J. Modi; pt. 2, ed. T. D. Anklesaria; ed. and trans. A. G. Perikhanian; trans. S. J. Bulsara.
MALIK b. Anas: trans. A. A. Bewley.
MANICHAEAN TEXTS (M, S): ed. M. Boyce.
MENOG I XRAD: ed. P. Sanjana.
MIHR YASHT: see Avesta; ed. and trans. I. Gershevitch.
NARSHAKHI: ed. M. Razavi; trans. R. N. Frye.
NERANGESTAN: ed. F. M. Kotwal and J. W. Boyd; ed. P. Sanjana; ed. and trans. A. Waag; ed. and trans. F. M. Kotwal and Ph. G. Kreyenbroek; trans. S. J. Bulsara.
OLD PERSIAN INSCRIPTIONS: ed. and trans. R. G. Kent.
PAHLAVI JAMASPI (Jamaspig): see Jamaspi.
PAHLAVI RIVAYAT ACCOMPANYING THE DADESTAN I DENIG: ed. B. N. Dhabar; ed. and trans. A. V. Williams.
PAHLAVI RIVAYAT OF ADURFARROBAY AND FARROBAYSROSH: ed. and trans. B. T. Anklesaria.
PAHLAVI TEXTS: ed. J. M. Jamasp-Asana.
PAHLAVI VISPERAD: ed. B. N. Dhabar.
PAHLAVI WENDIDAD (Videvdad): ed. and trans. B. T. Anklesaria.
PAHLAVI YASN (Yasna): ed. B. N. Dhabar.
PAZAND JAMASPI: see Jamaspi.
PERSEPOLIS FORTIFICATION TABLETS: ed. and trans. R. T. Hallock.
PERSEPOLIS TREASURY TABLETS: ed. and trans. G. G. Cameron.
PERSIAN JAMASPI: see Jamaspi.
PERSIAN REVAYATS: ed. M. R. Unvala; trans. B. N. Dhabar.
PLATO, Alcibiades: ed. and trans. W. R. M. Lamb.
PLUTARCH, Parallel Lives: ed. and trans. B. Perrin.
QABUS NAMA: trans. R. Levy.
QUR'AN: ed. and trans. M. M. Pickthall.
REHBAR-E DIN-E JARTHUSHTI: E. S. Meherjirana.

RIVAYAT I EMED I ASHAWAHISHTAN: ed. B. T. Anklesaria; ed. and trans. N. Safa-Isfehani.
SADDAR BONDAHESH: ed. B. N. Dhabar.
SEYASAT NAMA OR SEYAR AL-MOLUK: ed. and trans. H. Darke.
SHAH NAMA: ed. È. E. Bertels and others; ed. Dj. Khaleghi-Motlagh; trans. R. Levy; trans. A. G. Warner and E. Warner.
SHAPUR I'S INSCRIPTION: ed. M. Back; ed. and trans. Ph. Huyse.
SHKAND GUMANIG WIZAR: ed. J. M. Jamasp-Asana and E. W. West; ed. and trans. J. de Menasce.
SIROZA: see Avesta.
SUPPLEMENTARY TEXTS TO THE SHAYEST NE SHAYEST: ed. and trans. F. M. Kotwal.
TABARI, JAMI' AL-BAYAN: ed. and trans. J. Cooper, W. F. Madelung, and A. Jones.
TABARI, TA'RIKH: ed. M. J. de Goeje and others; trans. E. Yarshater and others.
TOSAR NAMA: ed. M. Minovi; trans. M. Boyce.
VAETHA NASK: ed. F. M. Kotwal; ed. and trans. H. Humbach and K. M. Jamaspasa.
VIDEVDAD: see Avesta, Pahlavi Wendidad.
VIS O RAMIN: trans. G. Morrison.
VISPERAD: see Avesta.
WIZIDAGIHA I ZADSPRAM: ed. and trans. B. T. Anklesaria; ed. and trans. M. Ph. Gignoux and A. Tafazzoli.
WIZIRIHA I DEN I WEH I MAZDESNAN: ed. and trans. K. M. Jamaspasa.
XENOPHON, Cyropaedia: ed. and trans. W. Miller.
XUSRO UD REDAG: ed. and trans. D. Monchi-Zadeh; ed. and trans. J. M. Unvala; trans. C. J. Brunner.
XWASTWANIFT: ed. and trans. J. P. Asmussen.
XWURDAG ABESTAG: see Avesta.
YASHTS: see Avesta; trans. H. Lommel.
YASNA: see Avesta.
YASNA HAPTANGHAITI: see Avesta; ed. and trans. J. Narten.
ZAND I WAHMAN YASN: ed. and trans. B. T. Anklesaria; ed. and trans. C. G. Cereti.
ZARDUXSHT NAMAG: ed. F. Rosenberg; ed. and trans. M. Molé.

References in this book usually are to the most recent date of publication or reissue. Note that spelling variations often occur in transcriptions of the titles of Indian, Iranian, Islamic, and Zoroastrian or Mazdean texts.

ALISHAN, LEONARDO P. 1989. "Sacred Archetypes and the Armenian Woman." *Journal of the Society for Armenian Studies* 4: 77–103.
AMORETTI, BIANCAMARIA S. 1975. "Sects and Heresies." In *The Cambridge History of Iran*. Vol. 3, ed. R. N. Frye, 481–519. Cambridge: Cambridge University Press.
ANKLESARIA, BEHRAMGORE T., ed. and trans. 1949. *Pahlavi Vendidad*. Bombay: K. R. Cama Oriental Institute.
———, ed. and trans. 1956. *Zand-Akasih: Iranian or Greater Bundahishn*. Bombay: Rahnumae Mazdayasnan Sabha.
———, ed. and trans. 1957. *Zand-i Vohuman Yasn and Two Pahlavi Fragments*. Bombay: K. L. Bhargava.
———, ed. 1962. *Rivayat-i Hemit-i Asavahistan*. Bombay: K. R. Cama Oriental Institute.
———, ed. and trans. 1964. *Vichitakiha-i Zatsparam*. Pt. 1. Bombay: Parsi Punchayet.
———, ed. and trans. 1969. *The Pahlavi Rivayat of Aturfarnbag and Farnbag-srosh*. 2 vols. Bombay: M. F. Cama Athornan Institute.
ANKLESARIA, PISHOTAN K., ed. 1958. "A Critical Edition of the Unedited Portion of the Datestan-i Denik." Ph.D. diss., School of Oriental and African Studies, University of London.
ANKLESARIA, TAHMURAS D., ed. 1899. *The Datistan-i Dinik*. Pt. 1. Bombay: Fort Printing Press.
———, ed. 1908. *The Bundahishn*. Bombay: British India Press.
———, ed. 1913. *Madigan-i-Hazar Dadistan*. Pt. 2. Bombay: Fort Printing Press.
ANTIA, EDALJI K., ed. and trans. 1900. *Karnamak-i Artakhshir Papakan*. Bombay: Fort Printing Press.
ASMUSSEN, JES P. 1965. *Xuastvanift: Studies in Manichaeism*. Copenhagen: Munksgaard.
———. 1974. "Some Remarks on Sasanian Demonology." In *Acta Iranica* 1, 236–241. Leiden: E. J. Brill.
———. 1982. "A Zoroastrian 'De-demonization' in Judeo-Persian." In *Irano-Judaica*. Vol. 1, ed. S. Shaked, 112–121. Jerusalem: Ben-Zvi Institute.
———. 1989. "Az." In *Encyclopaedia Iranica* 3, 168–169. London:

Routledge and Kegan Paul.

AUERBACH, NINA. 1982. *Woman and the Demon: The Life of a Victorian Myth*. Cambridge, Massachusetts: Harvard University Press.

AWN, PETER J. 1983. *Satan's Tragedy and Redemption: Iblis in Sufi Psychology*. Leiden: E. J. Brill.

AXELROD, PAUL. 1974. "A Social and Demographic Comparison of Parsis, Saraswat Brahmins, and Jains in Bombay." Ph.D. diss., Department of Anthropology, University of North Carolina.

AZARPAY, GUITTY. 1976. "The Allegory of Den in Persian Art." *Artibus Asiae* 38, 1: 37–48.

———. 1981. *Sogdian Painting: The Pictorial Epic in Oriental Art*. Berkeley: University of California Press.

BACK, MICHAEL, ed. 1978. *Die sassanidischen Staatsinschriften*. Acta Iranica 18. Leiden: E. J. Brill.

BAHAR, MEHRDAD, trans. 1991. *Bondahesh*. Tehran: Tus Publications.

BAILEY, HAROLD W. 1967. "Saka s's'andramata." In *Festschrift für Wilhelm Eilers*, 136–143. Wiesbaden: Otto Harrassowitz.

BARTHOLOMAE, CHRISTIAN. [1904] 1979. *Altiranisches Wörterbuch*. Berlin: Walter de Gruyter.

BEDUHN, JASON D. 2000. *The Manichaean Body: In Discipline and Ritual*. Baltimore: Johns Hopkins University Press.

BEN SHEMESH, AARON, trans. 1969. *Kitab al-kharaj*, by Ya'qub b. Ibrahim al-Ansari Abu Yusuf. Leiden: E. J. Brill.

BERTELS, ÈVGENII E., AND OTHERS, ed. 1960–1971. *Shah nama*, by Abu 'l-Qasem Ferdowsi. 9 vols. Moscow: Oriental Institute of the Soviet Academy of Sciences.

BEWLEY, AISHA A., trans. 1989. *al-Muwatta'*, by Malik b. Anas. London: Kegan Paul.

BIER, CAROL. 1985. "Anahid. ii. Anahita in the Arts." In *Encyclopaedia Iranica* 1, 1009–1011. London: Routledge and Kegan Paul.

BILLIMORIA, BEHRAM. N.d. "The Parsees in Ceylon." N.p.

BIRD, PHYLLIS. 1974. "Images of Woman in the Old Testament." In *Religion and Sexism: Images of Woman in the Jewish and Christian Traditions*, ed. R. R. Ruether, 41–88. New York: Simon and Schuster.

BISHOP, DALE. 1987. "When Gods Become Demons." In *Monsters and Demons in the Ancient and Medieval Worlds: Papers Presented in Honor of Edith Porada*, ed. A. E. Farkas, P. O. Harper, and E. B. Harrison, 95–100. Mainz: Philipp von Zabern.

BOARDMAN, JOHN. 2000. *Persia and the West: An Archaeological Investigation of the Genesis of Achaemenid Art*. London: Thames and

Hudson.

BOAS, FRANZ. 1940. "The Limitations of the Comparative Method in Anthropology." In *Race, Language, and Culture*, ed. F. Boaz, 270–280. New York: Macmillan.

BORISOV, ANDREI Y., AND VLADIMIR G. LUKONIN. 1963. *Sasanidskie Gemmy*. Leningrad: Izd-vo Gosudarstvennyi Ermitazha.

BOWMAN, RAYMOND A., ed. and trans. 1970. *Aramaic Ritual Texts from Persepolis*. Oriental Institute Publications 91. Chicago: University of Chicago Press.

BOYCE, MARY. 1968a. "Middle Persian Literature." In *Handbuch der Orientalistik*. Div. 1, Vol. 4, Sec. 2, Pt. 1, ed. B. Spuler, 31–66. Leiden: E. J. Brill.

———, trans. 1968b. *The Letter of Tansar*. Rome: Istituto Italiano per il Medio ed Estremo Oriente.

———, ed. 1975. *Manichaean Texts*, as *A Reader in Manichaean Middle Persian and Parthian*. Acta Iranica 9. Leiden: E. J. Brill.

———. 1977. *A Persian Stronghold of Zoroastrianism*. Oxford: Claredon Press.

———. 1979. *Zoroastrians: Their Religious Beliefs and Practices*. London: Routledge and Kegan Paul.

———. 1982. *A History of Zoroastrianism*. Vol. 2. Leiden: E. J. Brill.

———. 1984. *Textual Sources for the Study of Zoroastrianism*. Manchester: Manchester University Press.

———. 1985a. "Ahura Mazda." In *Encyclopaedia Iranica* 1, 684–687. London: Routledge and Kegan Paul.

———. 1985b. "Amurdad." In *Encyclopaedia Iranica* 1, 997–998. London: Routledge and Kegan Paul.

———. 1987. "Armaiti." In *Encyclopaedia Iranica* 2, 413–415. London: Routledge and Kegan Paul.

———. 1988a. "The Lady and the Scribe: Some Further Reflections on Anahit and Tir." In *A Green Leaf: Papers in Honour of Professor Jes P. Asmussen*, Acta Iranica 28, 277–282. Leiden: E. J. Brill.

———. 1988b. "The Religion of Cyrus the Great." In *Achaemenid History III: Method and Theory*, ed. A. Kuhrt and H. Sancisi-Weerdenburg, 15–31. Leiden: Nederlands Instituut voor het Nabije Oosten.

———. [1975] 1989. *A History of Zoroastrianism*. Vol. 1. 2d ed. Leiden: E. J. Brill.

———. 1991. "The 'Parsis' or Persians of Anatolia." In *K. R. Cama Oriental Institute Platinum Jubilee Volume*, 43–53. Bombay: K. R. Cama Oriental Institute.

―――. 1992. *Zoroastrianism: Its Antiquity and Constant Vigour*. Costa Mesa: Mazda Publishers.
BOYCE, MARY, AND FRANTZ GRENET. 1991. *A History of Zoroastrianism*. Vol. 3. Leiden: E. J. Brill.
BROCK, SEBASTIAN P., AND SUSAN A. HARVEY. 1987. *Holy Women of the Syrian Orient*. Berkeley: University of California Press.
BROSIUS, MARIA. 1996. *Women in Ancient Persia: 559–331 B.C.* Oxford: Clarendon Press.
―――. 1998. "Artemis Persike and Artemis Anaitis." In *Achaemenid History XI: Studies in Persian History*, ed. M. Brosius and A. Kuhrt, 227–238. Leiden: Nederlands Instituut voor het Nabije Oosten.
BROWN, PETER. 1988. *The Body and Society: Men, Women, and Sexual Renunciation in Early Christianity*. New York: Columbia University Press.
BROWNE, EDWARD G. [1893] 1984. *A Year Among the Persians*. London: Century Publishing Company.
BRUNNER, CHRISTOPHER J., trans. 1978. "Khusraw, Son of Kawad, and a Page." *Selected Texts for Pre-Islamic Iran*, Special Supplement to the Grapevine, 7–10.
BRUNT, PETER A., ed. and trans. 1983–1989. *Anabasis Alexandri*, by Arrian. Loeb Classical Library. Vols. 236, 269. Cambridge, Massachusetts: Harvard University Press.
BUCHANAN, CONSTANCE H. 1987. "Women's Studies." In *The Encyclopedia of Religion* 15, 433–440. New York: Macmillan.
BULLIET, RICHARD W. 1979. *Conversion to Islam in the Medieval Period: An Essay in Quantitative History*. Cambridge, Massachusetts: Harvard University Press.
―――. 1990. "Conversion Stories in Early Islam." In *Conversion and Continuity: Indigenous Christian Communities in Islamic Lands Eighth to Eighteenth Centuries*, ed. M. Gervers and R. J. Bikhazi, 123–133. Toronto: Pontifical Institute of Mediaeval Studies.
―――. 1994. *Islam: The View from the Edge*. New York: Columbia University Press.
BULSARA, SOHRAB J., trans. 1915. *Aerpatastan and Nirangastan*. Bombay: British India Press.
―――, trans. 1937. *Madayan i Hazar Dadestan*, as *The Laws of the Ancient Persians*. Bombay: Fort Printing Press.
BURKERT, WALTER. 1987. *Ancient Mystery Cults*. Cambridge, Massachusetts: Harvard University Press.
BURROW, THOMAS. 1973. "The Proto-Indoaryans." *Journal of the Royal*

Asiatic Society, 123–140.
BUTLER, JUDITH P. [1990] 1999. *Gender Trouble: Feminism and the Subversion of Identity*. London: Routledge.
BUTLER, MARILYN. 1989. "Repossessing the Past: The Case for an Open Literary History." In *Rethinking Historicism: Critical Readings in Romantic History*, ed. M. Levinson, M. Butler, J. McGann, and P. Hamilton, 64–84. Oxford: Basil Blackwell.
BYNUM, CAROLINE W. 1986a. "Introduction: The Complexity of Symbols." In *Gender and Religion: On the Complexity of Symbols*, ed. C. W. Bynum, S. Harrell, and P. Richman, 1–20. Boston: Beacon Press.
———. 1986b. "'... And Woman His Humanity': Female Imagery in the Religious Writing of the Later Middle Ages." In *Gender and Religion: On the Complexity of Symbols*, ed. C. W. Bynum, S. Harrell, and P. Richman, 257–288. Boston: Beacon Press.
CAMERON, GEORGE G., ed. and trans. 1948. *Persepolis Treasury Tablets*. Oriental Institute Publications 65. Chicago: University of Chicago Press.
CARTER, ELIZABETH. 1994. "Bridging the Gap between the Elamites and the Persians in Southeastern Khuzistan." In *Achaemenid History VIII: Continuity and Change*, ed. H. Sancisi-Weerdenburg, A. Kuhrt, and M. C. Root, 65–95. Leiden: Nederlands Instituut voor het Nabije Oosten.
CERETI, CARLO G., ed. and trans. 1995. *The Zand i Wahman Yasn: A Zoroastrian Apocalypse*. Serie Orientale Roma 75. Rome: Istituto per il Medio ed Estremo Oriente.
CHACHA, HOMI F., ed. and trans. 1936. *Gajastak Abalis*. Bombay: Parsi Punchayet.
CHAUMONT, MARIE LOUISE. 1985. "Anahid. ii. The Cult and Its Diffusion." In *Encyclopaedia Iranica* 1, 1006–1009. London: Routledge and Kegan Paul.
———. 1990. "Boran." In *Encyclopaedia Iranica* 4, 366. London: Routledge and Kegan Paul.
CHINIWALLA, FRAMROZE S. 1942. *Essential Origins of Zoroastrianism: Some Glimpses of the Mazdayasni Zarathoshti Daen in Its Original Native Light of Khshnoom*. Bombay: Parsi Vegetarian and Temperance Society.
CHOKSY, JAMSHEED K. 1986. "An Annotated Index of the Greater or Iranian Bundahishn (TD 2)." *Studia Iranica* 15, 2: 203–242.
———. 1987. "Zoroastrians in Muslim Iran: Selected Problems of Coexistence and Interaction During the Early Medieval Period." *Iranian Studies* 20, 1: 17–30.
———. 1988a. "Woman in the Zoroastrian Book of Primal Creation:

Images and Functions within a Religious Tradition." *The Mankind Quarterly* 29, 1–2: 73–82.

———. 1988b. "Sacral Kingship in Sasanian Iran." *Bulletin of the Asia Institute*, new series, 2: 35–52.

———. 1989a. *Purity and Pollution in Zoroastrianism: Triumph over Evil.* Austin: University of Texas Press.

———. 1989b. "A Sasanian Monarch, His Queen, Crown Prince, and Deities: The Coinage of Wahram II." *American Journal of Numismatics*, second series, 1: 117–135.

———. 1990. "Gesture in Ancient Iran and Central Asia II: Proskynesis and the Bent Forefinger." *Bulletin of the Asia Institute*, new series, 4: 201–207.

———. 1996. "Doctrinal Variation in Zoroastrianism: The Notion of Dualism." In *Second International Congress Proceedings*, 96–110. Bombay: K. R. Cama Oriental Institute.

———. 1997. *Conflict and Cooperation: Zoroastrian Subalterns and Muslim Elites in Medieval Iranian Society.* New York: Columbia University Press.

———. 1998. "Zoroastrianism." In *How Different Religions View Death and Afterlife.* 2d ed., ed. C. J. Johnson and M. G. McGee, 246–263. Philadelphia: Charles Press.

———. Forthcoming. *Earliest Zoroastrianism: An Archaeological and Textual Study.* Bombay: K. R. Cama Oriental Institute.

CHRISTENSEN, ARTHUR. 1917. *Les types du premier homme et du premier roi dans l'histoire légendaire des iraniens.* Vol. 1. Stockholm: Norstedt.

———. 1928. *Études sur le zoroastrisme de la perse antique.* Copenhagen: Munksgaard.

———. 1941. *Essai sur la démonologie iranienne.* Copenhagen: Munksgaard.

CLARK, ELIZABETH A. 1986. "Devil's Gateway and Bride of Christ: Women in the Early Christian World." In *Ascetic Piety and Women's Faith: Essays on Late Ancient Christianity.* By E. A. Clark, 23–60. Lewiston, New York: Edwin Mellen Press.

———. 1998. "The Lady Vanishes: Dilemmas of a Feminist Historian after the 'Linguistic Turn.'" *Church History* 67: 1–31.

COLLEDGE, MALCOLM A. R. 1977. *Parthian Art.* Ithaca: Cornell University Press.

———. 1986. *Iconography of Religions: The Parthian Period.* Leiden: E. J. Brill.

COLPE, CARSTEN. 1983. "Development of Religious Thought." In *The Cambridge History of Iran.* Vol. 3, Pt. 2, ed. E. Yarshater, 819–865.

Cambridge: Cambridge University Press.
CONRAD, PETER. 1999. *Modern Times, Modern Places.* New York: Alfred A. Knopf.
COOK, JOHN M. 1983. *The Persian Empire.* London: J. M. Dent.
——. 1985. "The Rise of the Achaemenids and Establishment of Their Empire." In *The Cambridge History of Iran.* Vol. 2, ed. I. Gershevitch, 200–291. Cambridge: Cambridge University Press.
COOPER, JOHN, WILFERD F. MADELUNG, AND ALAN JONES, ed. and trans. 1987. *Jami' al-bayan 'an ta'wil ay al-Qur'an,* by Abu Ja'far Muhammad b. Jarir al-Tabari. Vol. 1. Oxford: Oxford University Press.
CUMONT, FRANZ. [1903] 1956. *The Mysteries of Mithra.* Trans. T. J. McCormack. New York: Dover Publications.
——. 1975. "The Dura Mithraeum." In *Mithraic Studies.* Vol. 1, ed. J. R. Hinnells, 151–214. Manchester: Manchester University Press.
DADACHANJI, FAREDUN K. [1980] 1986. *Parsis Ancient and Modern and Their Religion.* Karachi: Ma'aref Printers.
DALEY, BRIAN E. 1999a. "Heaven." In *Late Antiquity: A Guide to the Postclassical World,* ed. G. W. Bowersock, P. Brown, and O. Grabar, 484–485. Cambridge: Massachusetts: Harvard University Press.
——. 1999b. "Hell." In *Late Antiquity: A Guide to the Postclassical World,* ed. G. W. Bowersock, P. Brown, and O. Grabar, 486–488. Cambridge: Massachusetts: Harvard University Press.
DANDAMAYEV, MUHAMMAD A. 1992. "Cassandane." In *Encyclopaedia Iranica* 5, 62. Costa Mesa: Mazda Publishers.
DANDAMAYEV, MUHAMMAD A., AND VLADIMIR G. LUKONIN. 1989. *The Culture and Social Institutions of Ancient Iran.* Cambridge: Cambridge University Press.
DANIELS, PETER T., AND WILLIAM BRIGHT, ed. 1996. *The World's Writing Systems.* New York: Oxford University Press.
DARKE, HUBERT, trans. 1960. *Siyasat nama or Siyar al-muluk,* by Nezam al-Molk, as *The Book of Government or Rules for Kings.* Boston: Routledge and Kegan Paul.
——, ed. 1962. *Siyar al-muluk or Siyasat nama,* by Nezam al-Molk. Tehran: B. T. N. K.
DARMESTETER, JAMES. 1892–1893. *Le Zend-Avesta.* 3 vols. Paris: Ernest Leroux.
DAVE, TRIMBAKLAL N. 1935. *A Study of the Gujarati Language in the 16th Century (v.s.).* London: Royal Asiatic Society.
DETIENNE, MARCEL. [1981] 1986. *The Creation of Mythology.* Trans. M. Cook. Chicago: University of Chicago Press.

DHABHAR, BAMANJI N., ed. 1909. *Saddar Nasr and Saddar Bundehesh: Persian Texts Relating to Zoroastrianism.* Bombay: Parsi Punchayet.
———, ed. 1913. *The Pahlavi Rivayat Accompanying the Dadistan-i Dinik.* Bombay: Parsi Punchayet.
———, ed. and trans. 1930. *Andarj-i-Aoshnar-i Danak.* Bombay: Parsi Punchayet.
———, trans. 1932. *The Persian Rivayats of Hormazyar Framarz and Others: Their Version with Introduction and Notes.* Bombay: K. R. Cama Oriental Institute.
———, ed. 1949. *Pahlavi Yasna and Visperad.* Bombay: Shahnamah Press.
DHALLA, MANECKJI N. [1942] 1975. *An Autobiography.* Trans. G. S. Rustomji and B. S. Rustomji. Karachi: Dastur Dhalla Memorial Institute.
DOTY, WILLIAM G. 1986. *Mythography: The Study of Myths and Rituals.* University, Alabama: University of Alabama Press.
DOUGLAS, MARY. [1966] 1969. *Purity and Danger: An Analysis of the Concepts of Pollution and Taboo.* London: Routledge and Kegan Paul.
———. [1970] 1982. *Natural Symbols: Explorations in Cosmology.* New York: Pantheon Books.
DRESDEN, MARK J., ed. 1966. *Denkart: A Pahlavi Text.* Wiesbaden: Otto Harrassowitz.
DUCHESNE-GUILLEMIN, JACQUES. 1966. *Symbols and Values in Zoroastrianism: Their Survival and Renewal.* New York: Harper and Row.
———. 1985a. "Ahriman." In *Encyclopaedia Iranica* 1, 670–673. London: Routledge and Kegan Paul.
———. 1985b. "There are More Things in Heaven and Earth." In *Orientalia Iosephi Tucci Memoriae Dicata.* Serie Orientale Roma 56, 1, ed. G. Gnoli and L. Lanciotti, 255–260. Rome: Istituto Italiano per il Medio ed Estremo Oriente.
DUMÉZIL, GEORGES. 1971. *The Destiny of a King.* Trans. A. Hiltebeitel. Chicago: University of Chicago Press.
DURKHEIM, ÉMILE. [1912] 1957. *The Elementary Forms of the Religious Life.* Trans. J. W. Swain. London: Georg Allen and Unwin.
EDULJEE, HOMI E. 1980. "The Date of Zoroaster." *Journal of the K. R. Cama Oriental Institute* 48: 103–160.
ELLIOTT, DYAN. 1999. *Fallen Bodies: Pollution, Sexuality, and Demonology in the Middle Ages.* Philadelphia: University of Pennsylvania Press.
FARAH, MADELAIN, trans. 1984. *Kitab adab al-nikah* from *Ihya' 'ulum al-din*, by Abu Hamid al-Ghazali, as *Marriage and Sexuality in Islam.* Salt Lake City: University of Utah Press.

FORSYTH, NEIL. [1987] 1989. *The Old Enemy: Satan and the Combat Myth*. Princeton: Princeton University Press.

FRYE, RICHARD N., trans. 1954. *Tarikh-i Bukhara*, by Abu Bakr Muhammad b. Ja'far al-Narshakhi, as *History of Bukhara*. Cambridge, Massachusetts: Mediaeval Academy of America.

———. 1975. *The Golden Age of Persia: Arabs in the East*. London: Weidenfeld and Nicolson.

———. 1984. *The History of Ancient Iran*. Munich: C. H. Beck.

———. 1985. "Zoroastrian Incest." In *Orientalia Iosephi Tucci Memoriae Dicata*. Serie Orientale Roma 56, 1, ed. G. Gnoli and L. Lanciotti, 445–455. Rome: Istituto Italiano per il Medio ed Estremo Oriente.

———. 1998. "Women in Pre-Islamic Central Asia: The Khatun of Bukhara." In *Women in the Medieval Islamic World: Power, Patronage, and Piety*, ed. G. R. G. Hambly, 55–68. New York: St. Martin's Press.

GAJENDRAGADKAR, S. N. 1974. *Parsi Gujarati: A Descriptive Analysis*. Bombay: University of Bombay Press.

GARDET, LOUIS. 1964. "Fitna." In *The Encyclopaedia of Islam*. 2d ed. 2, 930–931. Leiden: E. J. Brill.

GARRISON, MARK. 1999. "Fire Altars." In *Encyclopaedia Iranica* 9, 613–619. New York: Bibliotheca Persica Press.

GEIGER, WILHELM. [1882] 1885–1886. *Civilization of the Eastern Iranians in Ancient Times*. Trans. P. Sanjana. 2 vols. London: Henry Frowde.

GELDNER, KARL F., ed. [1886–1895] 1982. *Avesta: The Sacred Books of the Parsis*. 3 vols. Delhi: Parimal Publications.

GERSHEVITCH, ILYA, ed. and trans. 1967. *The Avestan Hymn to Mithra*. Cambridge: Cambridge University Press.

———. 1995. "Approaches to Zoroaster's Gathas." *Iran* 33: 1–29.

GIGNOUX, M. PHILIPPE. 1968. "L'enfer et le paradis d'après les sources pehlevies." *Journal asiatique* 256, 2: 219–245.

———, ed. and trans. 1984. *Le Livre d'Arda Viraz*. Paris: Editions Recherché sur les Civilisations.

———. 1989. "Azarmigduxt." In *Encyclopaedia Iranica* 3, 190. London: Routledge and Kegan Paul.

———, ed. and trans. 1991. *Les quatre inscriptions du mage Kirdir*. Studia Iranica cahier 9. Louvain: Peeters.

———. 1996. "Denag." In *Encyclopaedia Iranica* 7, 282. Costa Mesa: Mazda Publishers.

GIGNOUX, M. PHILIPPE, AND AHMAD TAFAZZOLI, ed. and trans. 1993. *Anthologie de Zadspram*. Studia Iranica cahier 13. Louvain: Peeters.

GINZBERG, LOUIS, ed. and trans. 1968. *Geonica*. 2d ed. New York: Hermon

Press.

GNOLI, GHERARDO. 1980. *Zoroaster's Time and Homeland*. Naples: Istituto Universitario Orientale.

———. 1987. "Ashtad." In *Encyclopaedia Iranica* 2, 826. London: Routledge and Kegan Paul.

———. 1989. *The Idea of Iran: An Essay on Its Origin*. Rome: Istituto Italiano per il Medio ed Estremo Oriente.

———. 1993. "A Sassanian Iconography of the Den." *Bulletin of the Asia Institute*, new series, 7: 79–85.

GÖBL, ROBERT. 1971. *Sasanian Numismatics*. Brunswick: Klinkhardt and Biermann.

———. 1984. *System und Chronologie der Münzprägung des Kushanreiches*. Vienna: Verlag der Österreichischen Akademie der Wissenschaften.

GODLEY, ALFRED D., ed. and trans. [1920–1925] 1981. *Herodotus*. Loeb Classical Library. Vols. 117–120. Cambridge, Massachusetts: Harvard University Press.

GOEJE, MICHAEL J. DE, ed. 1866. *Kitab futuh al-buldan*, by Ahmad b. Yahya al-Baladhuri. Leiden: E. J. Brill.

GOEJE, MICHAEL J. DE, AND OTHERS, ed. 1879–1901. *Ta'rikh al-rusul wa 'l-muluk*, by Abu Ja'far Muhammad b. Jarir al-Tabari. 3 ser., 15 vols. Leiden: E. J. Brill.

GORDON, RICHARD. 1996. *Image and Value in the Graeco-Roman World: Studies in Mithraism and Religious Art*. Brookfield, Vermont: Ashgate Publishing.

GOSSMAN, LIONEL. 1990. *Between History and Literature*. Cambridge: Massachusetts: Harvard University Press.

GOULD, KETAYUN H. 1994. "Outside the Discipline, Inside the Experience: Women in Zoroastrianism." In *Religion and Women*, ed. A. Sharma, 139–182. Albany: State University of New York Press.

GRABAR, OLEG, AND OTHERS. 1967. *Sasanian Silver: Late Antique and Early Mediaeval Arts of Luxury from Iran*. Ann Arbor: University of Michigan Museum of Art.

GRAINGER, JOHN D. 1997. *A Seleukid Prosopography and Gazetteer*. Leiden: E. J. Brill.

GRAY, LOUIS H. 1929. *The Foundations of the Iranian Religions*. Bombay: K. R. Cama Oriental Institute.

GRENET, FRANTZ, AND ZHANG GUANGDA. 1998. "The Last Refuge of the Sogdian Religion: Dunhuang in the Ninth and Tenth Centuries." *Bulletin of the Asia Institute*, new series, 10: 175–186.

GUIDI, IGNAZIO, ed. [1903] 1960. *Chronica minora*. Pt. 1. Corpus

Scriptorum Christianorum Orientalium. Scriptores Syri 1. Louvain: Secrétariat du CorpusSCO.

HALLOCK, RICHARD T., ed. and trans. 1969. *Persepolis Fortification Tablets*. Oriental Institute Publications 92. Chicago: University of Chicago Press.

——. 1985. "The Evidence of the Persepolis Tablets." In *The Cambridge History of Iran*. Vol. 2, ed. I. Gershevitch, 588–609. Cambridge: Cambridge University Press.

HAMBLY, GAVIN R. G. 1991. "The Pahlavi Autocracy: Riza Shah 1921–41." In *The Cambridge History of Iran*. Vol. 7, ed. P. Avery, G. R. G. Hambly, and C. Melville, 213–243. Cambridge: Cambridge University Press.

HARPER, PRUDENCE O. 1971. "Sources of Certain Female Representations in Sasanian Art." In *La Persia nel Medioevo*, 503–515. Rome: Accademia Nazionale dei Lincei.

——. 1978. *The Royal Hunter: Art of the Sasanian Empire*. New York: Asia Society.

HARPER, PRUDENCE O., AND PIETER MEYERS. 1981. *Silver Vessels in the Sasanian Period*. Vol. 1. New York: Metropolitan Museum of Art.

HAUG, MARTIN, AND HOSHANGJI J. ASA, ed. and trans. 1872. "Hadokht-Nask." In *The Book of Arda Viraf*, ed. and trans. M. Haug and H. J. Asa, 267–316. London: Trübner.

HENNING, WALTER B. 1951. *Zoroaster: Politician or Witch-Doctor?* London: Oxford University Press.

HERZFELD, ERNEST. 1947. *Zoroaster and His World*. 2 vols. Princeton: Princeton University Press.

HIEBERT, FREDRIK T., AND CLIFFORD C. LAMBERG-KARLOVSKY. 1992. "Central Asia and the Indo-Iranian Borderlands." *Iran* 30: 1–15.

HINNELLS, JOHN R. 1978. "Parsis and the British." *Journal of the K. R. Cama Oriental Institute* 46: 1–92.

——. 1981. *Zoroastrianism and the Parsis*. London: Ward Lock Educational.

——. 1983. "Social Change and Religious Transformation Among Bombay Parsis in the Early Twentieth Century." In *Traditions in Contact and Change*, ed. P. Slater and D. Wiebe, 105–125. Winnipeg: University of Manitoba Press.

——. 1996. *Zoroastrians in Britain*. Oxford: Clarendon Press.

HJERRILD, BODIL. 1988. "Zoroastrian Divorce." In *A Green Leaf: Papers in Honour of Professor Jes P. Asmussen*, Acta Iranica 28, 63–71. Leiden: E. J. Brill.

HJERRILD CARLSEN, BODIL. 1984. "The Cakar Marriage Contract and the

Cakar Children's Status in Matiyan i Hazar Datistan and Rivayat i Emet i Ashavahishtan." *Orientalia Lovaniensia Analecta* 16: 103–114.

HOFFMAN, KARL. 1965. "Av. daxma-." *Zeitschrift für vergleichende Sprachforschung* 79, 3–4: 238.

———. 1970. "Zur avestischen Textkritik: der Akk. Pl. mask. der a-Stämme." In *W. B. Henning Memorial Volume*, ed. M. Boyce and I. Gershevitch, 187–200. London: Lund Humphries.

HOPKINS, KEITH. 1980. "Brother-Sister Marriage in Roman Egypt." *Comparative Studies in Society and History* 22: 303–354.

HUDE, CAROLUS, ed. [1927] 1986. *Herodoti Historiae*. 3d ed. 2 vols. Oxford: Oxford University Press.

HUMBACH, HELMUT, ed. and trans. 1991. *The Gathas of Zarathushtra and the Other Old Avestan Texts*. 2 vols. Heidelberg: Carl Winter.

———. 1996. "Jamsheed in the Gathas and the Pahlavi Texts." In *Proceedings of the Second North American Gatha Conference*, ed. S. J. H. Manekshaw and P. R. Ichaporia, 71–85. Womelsdorf, Pennsylvania: Federation of Zoroastrian Associations of North America.

———. 2000. "The Meaning of Mazda and Ahura in the Gatha." *Iran Zamin* 1, 1: 29.

HUMBACH, HELMUT, AND JOSEF ELFENBEIN, ed. and trans. 1990. *Erbedestan: An Avesta-Pahlavi Text*. Munich: R. Kitzinger.

HUMBACH, HELMUT, AND PALLAN R. ICHAPORIA, ed. and trans. 1994. *The Heritage of Zarathushtra: A New Translation of His Gathas*. Heidelberg: Carl Winter.

HUMBACH, HELMUT, AND KAIKHUSROO M. JAMASPASA, ed. and trans. 1969. *Vaetha Nask: An Apocryphal Text on Zoroastrian Problems*. Wiesbaden: Otto Harrassowitz.

HUYSE, PHILIP, ed. and trans. 1999. *Die dreisprachige Inschrift Shabuhrs I. an der Ka'ba-i Zardusht*. 2 vols. Corpus Inscriptionum Iranicarum 3, 1. London: University of London School of Oriental and African Studies.

IBRAHIM, ASMA. 2001. "The Mystery of the 'Mummy'." *The Archaeological Review* (Pakistan) 8–10: 17–37.

INSLER, STANLEY, ed. and trans. 1975. *The Gathas of Zarathustra*. Acta Iranica 8. Leiden: E. J. Brill.

IQBAL, ABBAS, ed. 1942. *Tarikh-i Tabaristan*, by Baha' al-Din Muhammad b. Hasan b. Esfandiyar. Tehran: Eastern Bookstore.

JAAFARI-DEHAGHI, MAHMOUD, ed. and trans. 1998. *Dadestan i Denig*. Pt. 1. Studia Iranica cahier 20. Louvain: Peeters.

JACKSON, A. V. WILLIAMS. 1899. *Zoroaster: The Prophet of Ancient Iran*. New York: Macmillan and Columbia University Press.

———. 1906. *Persia Past and Present: A Book of Travel and Research.* New York: Macmillan.

———. 1923. "Studies in Manichaeism." *Journal of the American Oriental Society* 43: 15–25.

———. 1928. *Zoroastrian Studies: The Iranian Religion and Various Monographs.* New York: Macmillan and Columbia University Press.

———. 1930. "A Sketch of the Manichaean Doctrine Concerning the Future Life." *Journal of the American Oriental Society* 50: 177–198.

JAFAREY, ALI A. 1991. "Women: Venerated and Victimized." *Parsiana* 13, 10: 29–34.

JAMASPASA, KAIKHUSROO M., ed. and trans. 1970. "The Pahlavi Text of Viciriha i Den i Veh i Mazdayasnan." In *W. B. Henning Memorial Volume*, ed. M. Boyce and I. Gershevitch, 201–218. London: Lund Humphries.

JAMASP-ASANA, JAMASPJI M., ed. 1913. *The Pahlavi Texts.* Bombay: Fort Printing Press.

JAMASP-ASANA, JAMASPJI M., AND EDWARD W. WEST, ed. 1887. *Shikand-Gumanik Vijar.* Bombay: Government Central Book Depot.

JAMES, WILLIAM. [1961] 1974. *The Varieties of Religious Experience: A Study in Human Nature.* New York: Macmillan.

JAMZADEH, LAAL, AND MARGARET MILLS. 1986. "Iranian Sofreh: From Collective to Female Ritual." In *Gender and Religion: On the Complexity of Symbols*, ed. C. W. Bynum, S. Harrell, and P. Richman, 23–65. Boston: Beacon Press.

JESSAWALLA, DOSEBAI C. 1911. *The Story of My Life.* Bombay: Times Press.

JONG, ALBERT DE. 1995. "Jeh the Primal Whore? Observations on Zoroastrian Misogyny." In *Female Stereotypes in Religious Traditions*, ed. R. Kloppenborg and W. J. Hanegraaff, 15–41. Leiden: E. J. Brill.

JUSTI, FERDINAND. 1895. *Iranisches Namenbuch.* Marburg: Elwert.

KANGA, MANECK F., ed. and trans. 1960. *Chitak Handarz i Poryotkeshan: A Pahlavi Text.* Bombay: Dorab H. Kanga.

———, trans. 1983. "Hadhokht Nask." *Noor-e-Dastagir* 1, 1: 11–15.

KARAKA, DOSABHOY F. 1858. *The Parsees: Their History, Manners, Customs, and Religion.* London: Smith, Elder.

KATRAK, JAMSHED C. 1965. *Marriage in Ancient Iran.* Bombay: N.p.

KAUFMANN, LINDA S, ed. 1989. *Gender and Theory: Dialogues on Feminist Criticism.* Oxford: Basil Blackwell.

KAWAMI, TRUDY S. 1987. *Monumental Art of the Parthian Period in Iran.* Acta Iranica 26. Leiden: E. J. Brill.

KELLENS, JEAN. 1987. "Artazostre." In *Encyclopaedia Iranica* 2, 660.

London: Routledge and Kegan Paul.
———. 1989. "Avesta." In *Encyclopaedia Iranica* 3, 35–44. London: Routledge and Kegan Paul.
———. 1996a. "The Written Period of Transmission of the Avesta." In *Proceedings of the Second North American Gatha Conference*, ed. S. J. H. Manekshaw and P. R. Ichaporia, 121–125. Womelsdorf, Pennsylvania: Federation of Zoroastrian Associations of North America.
———. 1996b. "Druj." In *Encyclopaedia Iranica* 7, 562–563. Costa Mesa: Mazda Publishers.
———. 1996c. "Drvaspa." In *Encyclopaedia Iranica* 7, 565. Costa Mesa: Mazda Publishers.
———. 2000. *Essays on Zarathustra and Zoroastrianism*. Ed. and trans. P. O. Skjærvø. Costa Mesa: Mazda Publishers.
KELLENS, JEAN, AND ERIC PIRART, ed. and trans. 1988–1991. *Les textes vieil-avestiques*. 3 vols. Wiesbaden: Ludwig Reichert Verlag.
KELLEY, RON, JONATHAN FRIEDLANDER, AND ANITA COLBY, ed. 1993. *Irangeles: Iranians in Los Angeles*. Berkeley: University of California Press.
KENT, ROLAND G., ed. and trans. [1953] 1982. *Old Persian: Grammar, Texts, Lexicon*. 2d ed. New Haven: American Oriental Society.
KEYDELL, RUDOLFUS, ed. 1967. *Agathiae Myrinaei: Historiarum Libri Quinque*. Berlin: Walter de Gruyter.
KHALEGHI-MOTLAGH, DJALAL, ed. 1988–. *Shah nama*, by Abu 'l-Qasem Ferdowsi. Persian Text Series, new series, 1. 5 volumes to date. New York: Bibliotheca Persica.
———. 1989. "Bar. i. From the Achaemenid through the Safavid Period." In *Encyclopaedia Iranica* 3, 731–734. London: Routledge and Kegan Paul.
KIRK, GEOFFREY S. [1970] 1973. *Myth: Its Meaning and Functions in Ancient and Other Cultures*. Cambridge: Cambridge University Press.
KLOPPENBORG, RIA. 1995. "Introduction." In *Female Stereotypes in Religious Traditions*, ed. R. Kloppenborg and W. J. Hanegraaff, vii–xii. Leiden: E. J. Brill.
KOCH, HEIDEMARIE. 1977. *Die religiösen Verhältnisse des Dareioszeit: Untersuchungen anhand der elamischen Persepolistäfelchen*. Wiesbaden: Otto Harrassowitz.
KOTWAL, FIROZE M., ed. 1966. *Edito Princeps of the Vaetha with Transcription of the Pahlavi Version*. Bombay: Dorab H. Kanga.
———, ed. and trans. 1969. *The Supplementary Texts to the Shayest ne-shayest*. Copenhagen: Munksgaard.

———. 1988. "Initiation into the Zoroastrian Priesthood: Present Parsi Practice and an Old Pahlavi Text." In *A Green Leaf: Papers in Honour of Professor Jes P. Asmussen*, Acta Iranica 28, 299–307. Leiden: E. J. Brill.

KOTWAL, FIROZE M., AND JAMES W. BOYD, ed. 1980. *Erbadistan ud Nirangistan: Facsimile Edition of the Manuscript TD*. Cambridge, Massachusetts: Harvard University Department of Near Eastern Languages and Civilizations.

KOTWAL, FIROZE M., AND PHILIP G. KREYENBROEK, ed. and trans. 1992. *The Herbedestan and Nerangestan*. Vol. 1. Studia Iranica cahier 10. Louvain: Peeters.

———, ed. and trans. 1995. *The Herbedestan and Nerangestan*. Vol. 2. Studia Iranica cahier 16. Louvain: Peeters.

KREYENBROEK, PHILIP G. 1993. "On Spenta Mainyu's Role in the Zoroastrian Cosmogony." *Bulletin of the Asia Institute*, new series, 7: 97–103.

KUIPER, FRANCISCUS B. J. 1964. "The Bliss of Asha." *Indo-Iranian Journal* 8: 96–129.

KULKE, ECKEHARD. 1974. *The Parsees in India: A Minority as Agent of Social Change*. Delhi: Vikas.

LAKOFF, GEORGE. 1987. *Women, Fire, and Dangerous Things: What Categories Reveal About the Mind*. Chicago: University of Chicago Press.

LAMB, WALTER R. M., ed. and trans. 1927. *Alcibiades*, by Plato. Loeb Classical Library. Vol. 201. Cambridge, Massachusetts: Harvard University Press.

LAMBERG-KARLOVSKY, CLIFFORD. Forthcoming. "Archaeology and Language: The Case of the Bronze Age Indo-Iranians." *Current Anthropology*.

LANGSTAFF, HILARY A. 1987. *Indian Parsis in the Twentieth Century*. Karachi: Informal Religious Meetings Trust Fund.

LANKARANY, FIROUZ-THOMAS. 1985. *Daena im Avesta: Eine semantische Untersuchung*. Reinbeck: Verlag für Orientalistische Fachpublikationen.

LERNER, GERDA. 1986. *The Creation of Patriarchy*. New York: Oxford University Press.

LEVENSON, JON D. 1988. *Creation and the Persistence of Evil: The Jewish Drama of Divine Omnipotence*. San Francisco: Harper and Row.

LEVINSON, MARJORIE. 1989a. "Introduction." In *Rethinking Historicism: Critical Readings in Romantic History*, ed. M. Levinson, M. Butler, J. McGann, and P. Hamilton, 1–17. Oxford: Basil Blackwell.

———. 1989b. "The New Historicism: Back to the Future." In *Rethinking Historicism: Critical Readings in Romantic History*, ed. M. Levinson,

M. Butler, J. McGann, and P. Hamilton, 18–63. Oxford: Basil Blackwell.

Lévi-Strauss, Claude. [1978] 1979. *Myth and Meaning.* New York: Schocken Books.

Levy, Reuben, trans. 1951. *Qabus nama,* by Kay Ka'us b. Eskandar, as *A Mirror for Princes.* London: Cresset Press.

———, trans. 1967. *Shah nama,* by Abu 'l-Qasem Ferdowsi, as *The Epic of Kings.* Persian Heritage Series 2. London: Routledge and Kegan Paul.

Lévy-Bruhl, Lucien. [1926] 1985. *How Natives Think.* Trans. L. A. Clare. Princeton: Princeton University Press.

Lewis, David M. 1990. "The Persepolis Fortification Texts." In *Achaemenid History IV: Centre and Periphery,* ed. H. Sancisi-Weerdenburg and A. Kuhrt, 1–6. Leiden: Nederlands Instituut voor het Nabije Oosten.

Lincoln, Bruce. 1981. *Emerging from the Chrysalis: Studies in Rituals of Women's Initiation.* Cambridge, Massachusetts: Harvard University Press.

Lommel, Herman, trans. 1927. *Die Yäsht's des Awesta.* Göttingen: Vandenhoeck and Ruprecht.

———. 1930. *Die Religion Zarathustras nach dem Awesta dargestellt.* Tübingen: J. C. B. Mohr.

Luhrmann, Tanya M. 1996. *The Good Parsi: The Fate of a Colonial Elite in a Postcolonial Society.* Cambridge, Massachusetts: Harvard University Press.

MacKenzie, David N. 1971. *A Concise Pahlavi Dictionary.* London: Oxford University Press.

MacKenzie, David N., and Anahit G. Perikhanian. 1969. "The Model Marriage Contract in Pahlavi with an Addendum." In *K. R. Cama Oriental Institute Golden Jubilee Volume,* 103–112. Bombay: K. R. Cama Oriental Institute.

Madan, Dhanjishah M., ed. 1911. *The Complete Text of the Pahlavi Dinkard.* 2 vols. Bombay: Society for the Promotion of Researches into the Zoroastrian Religion.

Malandra, William W. 1983. *An Introduction to Ancient Iranian Religion: Readings from the Avesta and Achaemenid Inscriptions.* Minneapolis: University of Minnesota Press.

———. 1996. "Archaism and History in Gathic Studies." In *Proceedings of the Second North American Gatha Conference,* ed. S. J. H. Manekshaw and P. R. Ichaporia, 139–152. Womelsdorf, Pennsylvania: Federation of Zoroastrian Associations of North America.

MANECK, SUSAN S. 1997. *The Death of Ahriman: Culture, Identity, and Theological Change among the Parsis of India.* Bombay: K. R. Cama Oriental Institute.

MARGLIN, FRÉDÉRIQUE A. 1987. "Hierodouleia." In *The Encyclopedia of Religion* 5, 309–313. New York: Macmillan.

MARKER, KEKOBAD A. 1985. *A Petal from the Rose.* 2 vols. Karachi: Rosette.

MATHIESEN, HANS E. 1992. *Sculpture in the Parthian Period: A Study in Chronology.* 2 vols. Aarhus: Aarhus University Press.

MCGANN, JEROME. 1989. "The Third World of Criticism." In *Rethinking Historicism: Critical Readings in Romantic History,* ed. M. Levinson, M. Butler, J. McGann, and P. Hamilton, 85–107. Oxford: Basil Blackwell.

MEHERJIRANA, ERACHJI S. [1869] 1982. *Rehbar-e Din-e Jarthushti.* Trans. F. M. Kotwal and J. W. Boyd as *A Guide to the Zoroastrian Religion: A Nineteenth Century Catechism with Modern Commentary.* Chico, California: Scholars Press.

MENANT, DELPHINE. [1898] 1994. *The Parsis.* Trans. M. M. Murzban and A. D. Mango. 3 vols. Bombay: Danai.

MENASCE, JEAN DE, ed. and trans. 1945. *Shkand-Gumanik Vicar: La solution décisive des doutes.* Fribourg: L'Université de Fribourg en Suisse.

———. 1967. "Problèmes des mazdéens dans l'Iran musulman." In *Festschrift für Wilhelm Eilers,* ed. G. Wiessner, 220–230. Wiesbaden: Otto Harrassowitz.

MERNISSI, FATIMA. 1987. *Beyond the Veil: Male-Female Dynamics in a Modern Muslim Society.* 2d ed. Bloomington: Indiana University Press.

MILLER, WALTER, ed. and trans. [1914] 1979–1983. *Cyropaedia,* by Xenophon. Loeb Classical Library. Vols. 51–52. Cambridge, Massachusetts: Harvard University Press.

MINNS, ELLIS H. 1915. "Parchments of the Parthian Period from Avroman in Kurdistan." *Journal of Hellenistic Studies* 35: 22–65.

MINOVI, MOJTABA, ed. 1932. *Tansar nama.* Tehran: Majles Printing House.

MISTREE, KHOJESTE P. 1982. *Zoroastrianism: An Ethnic Perspective.* Bombay: Zoroastrian Studies.

———. 1990. "The Breakdown of the Zoroastrian Tradition as Viewed from a Contemporary Perspective." In *Irano-Judaica.* Vol. 2, ed. S. Shaked and A. Netzer, 227–254. Jerusalem: Ben Zvi Institute.

MOAYYAD, HESHMAT. 1988. "Lyric Poetry." In *Persian Literature,* ed. E. Yarshater, 120–146. New York: Bibliotheca Persica.

MODI, JIVANJI J., ed. 1901. *Madigan-i-Hazar Dadistan.* Bombay: Parsi Panchayet.

———, ed. and trans. 1903. *Jamaspi: Pahlavi, Pazend, and Persian Texts.* Bombay: Education Society.

———, ed. and trans. 1924. *The Persian Farziat-Nameh and Kholaseh-i Din of Dastur Darab Pahlan.* Bombay: Fort Printing Press.

MOLÉ, MARIJAN. 1963. *Culte, mythe et cosmologie dans l'Iran ancien. Le problème zoroastrien et la tradition mazdéenne.* Paris: Presses Universitaires de France.

———, ed. and trans. 1967. *La légende de Zoroastre. Selon les textes pehlevis.* Paris: Libraire C. Klincksieck.

MONCHI-ZADEH, DAVOUD, ed. and trans. 1982. "Xusrov i Kavatan ut Retak." In *Monumentum Georg Morgenstierne II,* Acta Iranica 22, 47–91. Leiden: E. J. Brill.

MOOREY, PETER R. S. 1988. "The Persian Empire." In *The Cambridge Ancient History.* Vol. 4, Pt. 2. 2d ed., ed. J. Boardman, 1–94. Cambridge: Cambridge University Press.

MOREEN, VERA B. 2000. *In Queen Esther's Garden: An Anthology of Judeo-Persian Literature.* New Haven: Yale University Press.

MORONY, MICHAEL G. 1984. *Iraq after the Muslim Conquest.* Princeton: Princeton University Press.

MORRISON, GEORGE, trans. 1972. *Vis and Ramin,* by Fakhr al-Din Gorgani. New York: Columbia University Press.

NARTEN, JOHANNA. 1982. *Die Amesha Spentas im Avesta.* Wiesbaden: Ludwig Reichert Verlag.

———, ed. and trans. 1986. *Der Yasna Haptanghaiti.* Wiesbaden: Ludwig Reichert Verlag.

NEUSNER, JACOB. 1986. *Judaism, Christianity, and Zoroastrianism in Talmudic Babylonia.* Lanham, Maryland: University Press of America.

New Oxford Annotated Bible with the Apocryphal and Deuterocanonical Books (New Revised Standard Version). [1991] 1994. New York: Oxford University Press.

NÖLDEKE, THEODOR. 1883. *Die von Guidi herausgegebene Syrische Chronik.* Sitzungsberichte der philosophisch-historischen Klasse der kaiserlichen Akademie der Wissenschaften 128. Vienna: Akademie der Wissenschaften.

NOSHIRWANI, MEHER M. 1990. *The Position of Women in Zoroastrianism.* Karachi: Shirkat Gah.

NYBERG, HENRIK S. [1938] 1966. *Die Religionen des alten Iran.* Osnabrück: O. Zeller.

———. 1974. *A Manual of Pahlavi.* Pt. 2. Wiesbaden: Otto Harrassowitz.

O'FLAHERTY, WENDY D. [1976] 1980. *The Origins of Evil in Hindu Mythology.* Berkeley: University of California Press.

———. [1980] 1982. *Women, Androgynes, and Other Mythical Beasts.* Chicago: University of Chicago Press.

PAGELS, ELAINE. 1988. *Adam, Eve, and the Serpent.* New York: Random House.

PALMER, ANDREW. 1990. *Monk and Mason on the Tigris Frontier: The Early History of Tur 'Abdin.* Cambridge: Cambridge University Press.

———, ed. and trans. 1993. *The Seventh Century in the West-Syrian Chronicles.* Liverpool: Liverpool University Press.

PALSETIA, JESSE S. 2001. *The Parsis of India: Preservation of Identity in Bombay City.* Leiden: E. J. Brill.

PANAINO, ANTONIO. 1996. "Duzhyairya." In *Encyclopaedia Iranica* 7, 615–616. Costa Mesa: Mazda Publishers.

———. 1997. "Nairika-e jahika- nell'aldilà zoroastriano." In *Bandhu. Scritti in onore di Carlo Della Casa.* Vol. 2, ed. R. Arena and others, 831–843. Alessandria: Edizioni dell'Orso.

PARSAY, FARROKHRO, HUMA AHI, AND MALEKE TALEQANI. 1977. *Zan dar Iran-e Bastan.* Tehran: Offset Press.

PAVRY, CURSETJI. 1929. *The Zoroastrian Doctrine of a Future Life.* 2d ed. New York: Columbia University Press.

PERIKHANIAN, ANAHIT G. 1970. "On Some Pahlavi Legal Terms." In *W. B. Henning Memorial Volume,* ed. M. Boyce and I. Gershevitch, 349–357. London: Lund Humphries.

———. 1983. "Iranian Society and Law." In *The Cambridge History of Iran.* Vol. 3, Pt. 2, ed. E. Yarshater, 627–680. Cambridge: Cambridge University Press.

———, ed. and trans. 1997. *The Book of a Thousand Judgments (A Sasanian Law-Book).* Trans. N. Garsoïan. Costa Mesa: Mazda Publishers.

PERRIN, BERNADOTTE, ed. and trans. [1914–1926] 1993. *Parallel Lives,* by Plutarch. Loeb Classical Library. Vols. 46–47, 65, 80, 87, 98–103. Cambridge, Massachusetts: Harvard University Press.

PICKTHALL, MUHAMMAD M., ed. and trans. 1977. *The Meaning of the Glorious Qur'an: Text and Explanatory Translation.* New York: Muslim World League.

PORADA, EDITH. [1962] 1965. *The Art of Ancient Iran: Pre-Islamic Cultures.* New York: Crown Publishers.

PULLEYBLANK, EDWIN G. 1992. "Chinese-Iranian Relations. i. In Pre-Islamic Times." In *Encyclopaedia Iranica* 5, 424–431. Costa Mesa: Mazda Publishers.

RAMANNA, MRIDULA. 1997. "A Voice from the Nineteenth Century: The Story of Dosebai Cowasjee." *Journal of the K. R. Cama Oriental*

Institute 61: 1–16.
RAZAVI, MUHAMMAD, ed. 1939. *Tarikh-i Bukhara*, by Abu Bakr Muhammad b. Ja'far al-Narshakhi. Tehran: Bonyad-e Farhang-e Iran.
RICOEUR, PAUL. [1967] 1969. *The Symbolism of Evil*. Boston: Beacon Press.
ROMEY, KRISTIN M., AND MARK ROSE. 2001. "Saga of the Persian Princess." *Archaeology* 54, 1: 24–25.
ROSE, JENNIFER. 1989. "The Traditional Role of Women in the Iranian and Indian (Parsi) Zoroastrian Communities from the Nineteenth to the Twentieth Century." *Journal of the K. R. Cama Oriental Institute* 56: 1–103.
———. 1998. "Three Queens, Two Wives, and A Goddess: Roles and Images of Women in Sasanian Iran." In *Women in the Medieval Islamic World: Power, Patronage, and Piety*, ed. G. R. G. Hambly, 29–54. New York: St. Martin's Press.
ROSENBERG, FREDERIC, ed. 1904. *Zarduxsht namag*, by Zardosht Bahram-i Pajdo, as *Zaratusht Nama: Le livre de Zoroastre*. St. Petersburg: Academie Imperial des Sciences.
RUSSELL, JAMES R. 1987. *Zoroastrianism in Armenia*. Harvard Iranian Series 5. Cambridge, Massachusetts: Harvard University Department of Near Eastern Languages and Civilizations.
———. 1990a. "Zoroastrian Elements in the Book of Esther." In *Irano-Judaica*. Vol. 2, ed. S. Shaked and A. Netzer, 36–40. Jerusalem: Ben Zvi Institute.
———. 1990b. "Chador. ii. Among Zoroastrians." In *Encyclopaedia Iranica* 4, 610. London: Routledge and Kegan Paul.
———. 1996. "New Materials Toward the Life of the Prophet Zarathushtra." In *Proceedings of the Second North American Gatha Conference*, ed. S. J. H. Manekshaw and P. R. Ichaporia, 197–215. Womelsdorf, Pennsylvania: Federation of Zoroastrian Associations of North America.
RUSSELL, JEFFREY B. 1986. *Mephistopheles: The Devil in the Modern World*. Ithaca: Cornell University Press.
———. [1981] 1987. *Satan: The Early Christian Tradition*. Ithaca: Cornell University Press.
———. [1977] 1988. *The Devil: Perceptions of Evil from Antiquity to Primitive Christianity*. Ithaca: Cornell University Press.
SAFA-ISFEHANI, NEZHAT, ed. and trans. 1980. *Rivayat-i Hemit-i Ashawahistan: A Study in Zoroastrian Law*. Harvard Iranian Series 2. Cambridge: Massachusetts: Harvard University Department of Near Eastern Languages and Civilizations.
SAHMI, HAMZA B. YUSUF AL-. 1967 edition. *Ta'rikh Jurjan wa kitab ma'rifat*

'ulama' ahl Jurjan. Hyderabad: Osmania Oriental Publications Bureau.
SANCISI-WEERDENBURG, HELEEN. [1983] 1993. "Exit Atossa: Images of Women in Greek Historiography on Persia." In *Images of Women in Antiquity*, 2d ed., ed. A. Cameron and A. Kuhrt, 20–33, 303. Detroit: Wayne State University Press.
SANJANA, PESHOTAN, ed. 1894. *Nirangistan*. Bombay: Parsi Punchayet.
———, ed. 1895. *The Dini i Maino i Khrat*. Bombay: Education Society.
———. 1932. "Position of Zoroastrian Women in Remote Antiquity." In *The Collected Works of the Late Dastur Darab Peshotan Sanjana*, 506–524. Bombay: British India Press.
SARIANIDI, VICTOR. 1998. *Margiana and Protozoroastrianism*. Trans. I. Sarianidi. Athens: Kapon Editions.
SAVRAMIS, DEMOSTHENES. 1974. *The Satanizing of Woman: Religion versus Sexuality*. Trans. M. Ebon. Garden City, New York: Doubleday.
SCHLERATH, BERNFRIED. 1985a. "Ahrishwang." In *Encyclopaedia Iranica* 1, 673–674. London: Routledge and Kegan Paul.
———. 1985b. "Ahurani." In *Encyclopaedia Iranica* 1, 688. London: Routledge and Kegan Paul.
SCHMIDT, ERICH F. 1939. *The Treasury of Persepolis and Other Discoveries in the Homeland of the Achaemenians*. Oriental Institute Communications 21. Chicago: University of Chicago Press.
———. 1953–1970. *Persepolis*. 3 vols. Oriental Institute Publications 68–70. Chicago: University of Chicago Press.
SCHMITT, RÜDIGER. 1985a. "Amytis." In *Encyclopaedia Iranica* 1, 999. London: Routledge and Kegan Paul.
———. 1985b. "Amestris." In *Encyclopaedia Iranica* 1, 936–937. London: Routledge and Kegan Paul.
———. 1987. "Artystone." In *Encyclopaedia Iranica* 2, 665. London: Routledge and Kegan Paul.
———. 1989a. "Atossa." In *Encyclopaedia Iranica* 3, 13–14. London: Routledge and Kegan Paul.
———, ed. 1989b. *Compendium linguarum Iranicarum*. Wiesbaden: Ludwig Reichert Verlag.
SCHWARTZ, MARTIN. 1985. "The Religion of Achaemenian Iran." In *The Cambridge History of Iran*. Vol. 2, ed. I. Gershevitch, 664–697. Cambridge: Cambridge University Press.
———. 1986. "Coded Sound Patterns, Acrostics, and Anagrams in Zoroaster's Oral Poetry." In *Studia Grammatica Iranica: Festschrift für Helmut Humbach*, ed. R. Schmitt and P. O. Skjærvø, 327–392. Munich: R. Kitzinger.

———. 1991. "Sound, Sense, and 'Seeing' in Zoroaster: The Outer Reaches of Orality." In *International Congress Proceedings*, 127–163. Bombay: K. R. Cama Oriental Institute.

SCOTT, JOAN W. 1988. *Gender and the Politics of History*. New York: Columbia University Press.

———. 1991. "The Evidence of Experience." *Critical Inquiry* 17: 773–797.

SEVENTH NORTH AMERICAN ZOROASTRIAN CONGRESS, 1990. *The Proceedings of the Unification Congress*. Houston: Zoroastrian Association of Houston.

SHAHBAZI, A. SHAPUR. 1977. "The 'Traditional Date of Zoroaster' Explained." *Bulletin of the School of Oriental and African Studies* 40, 1: 25–35.

———. 1983. "Studies in Sasanian Prosopography." *Archaeologische Mitteilungen aus Iran* 16: 255–268.

———. 1987. "Apama." In *Encyclopaedia Iranica* 2, 150. London: Routledge and Kegan Paul.

SHAHROKH, SHAHROKH, AND RASHNA WRITER, ed. and trans. 1994. *The Memoirs of Keikhosrow Shahrokh*. Lewiston: Edwin Mellen Press.

SHAKED, SHAUL. 1967. "Some Notes on Ahreman, the Evil Spirit, and His Creation." In *Studies in Mysticism and Religion Presented to Gershom G. Scholem*, 227–234. Jerusalem: Magnes Press.

———. 1982. "Two Judaeo-Iranian Contributions." In *Irano-Judaica*. Vol. 1, ed. S. Shaked, 292–322. Jerusalem: Ben-Zvi Institute.

SHAKI, MANSOUR. 1971. "The Sasanian Matrimonial Relations." *Archív orientální* 39: 322–345.

———. 1988. "Pahlavica." In *A Green Leaf: Papers in Honour of Professor Jes P. Asmussen*, Acta Iranica 28, 93–99. Leiden: E. J. Brill.

———. 1989. "Ayoken." In *Encyclopaedia Iranica* 3, 149. London: Routledge and Kegan Paul.

———. 1990. "Chakar." In *Encyclopaedia Iranica* 4, 647–649. London: Routledge and Kegan Paul.

———. 1996. "Den." In *Encyclopaedia Iranica* 7, 279–281. Costa Mesa: Mazda Publishers.

———. 1999. "Family Law. i. In Zoroastrianism" In *Encyclopaedia Iranica* 9, 184–189. New York: Bibliotheca Persica Press.

SHARMA, ARVIND, ed. 1987. *Women in World Religions*. Albany: State University of New York Press.

SKJÆRVØ, P. OKTOR. 1983. "'Kirdir's Vision': Translation and Analysis." *Archaeologische Mitteilungen aus Iran* 16: 269–306.

———. 1994. "Hymnic Composition in the Avesta." *Die Sprache* 36:

199–244.

———. 1995. "Iranian Elements in Manicheism: A Comparative Contrastive Approach. Irano-Manichaica I." In *Au carrefour des religions: Mélanges offerts à Philippe Gignoux*, ed. R. Gyselen, 263–284. Bures-sur-Yvette: Groupe pour l'Étude de la Civilisation du Moyen-Orient.

———. 1996. "The Literature of the Most Ancient Iranians." In *Proceedings of the Second North American Gatha Conference*, ed. S. J. H. Manekshaw and P. R. Ichaporia, 221–235. Womelsdorf, Pennsylvania: Federation of Zoroastrian Associations of North America.

———. 1997. "The State of Old Avestan Scholarship." *Journal of the American Oriental Society* 117, 1: 103–114.

SMITH, JANE I., AND YVONNE Y. HADDAD. 1981. *The Islamic Understanding of Death and Resurrection*. Albany: State University of New York Press.

SPELLBERG, DENISE A. 1988. "Nizam al-Mulk's Manipulation of Tradition: 'Aisha and the Role of Women in Islamic Government." *The Muslim World* 78, 2: 111–117.

SPYCKET, AGNES. 1980. "Women in Persian Art." In *Ancient Persia: The Art of an Empire*, ed. D. Schmandt-Besserat, 43–45. Malibu, California: Undena Publications.

STRONACH, DAVID. 1978. *Pasargadae*. Oxford: Clarendon Press.

SUMNER, WILLIAM. 1994. "Archaeological Measures of Cultural Continuity and the Arrival of the Persians in Fars." In *Achaemenid History VIII: Continuity and Change*, ed. H. Sancisi-Weerdenburg, A. Kuhrt, and M. C. Root, 97–105. Leiden: Nederlands Instituut voor het Nabije Oosten.

SUNDERMANN, WERNER. 1978. "Some More Remarks on Mithra in the Manichaean Pantheon." In *Études Mithriaques*, Acta Iranica 17, 485–499. Leiden: E. J. Brill.

———. 1994. "Eva illuminatrix." In *Gnosisforschung und Religionsgeschichte: Festschrift für Kurt Rudolph zum 65. Geburtstag*, ed. H. Preißler and H. Seiwert, 317–327. Marburg: Diagonal-Verlag.

Tanakh: A New Translation of the Holy Scriptures According to the Traditional Hebrew Text. 1985. Philadelphia: Jewish Publication Society.

TARAPOREWALA, IRACH J. S. 1937. "The Ideal Aryan Womanhood." In *The Young Man's Zoroastrian Association of Karachi Silver Jubilee Volume 1910–1935*, 69–75. Karachi: Silver Jubilee Committee.

TAVARIA, PHIROZ N. 1971. *A Manual of Khshnoom: The Zoroastrian Occult Knowledge*. Bombay: Parsi Vegetarian and Temperance Society.

TIRMIDHI, ABU 'ISA MUHAMMAD AL-. 1964–1968 edition. *Jami' al-sahih*. 5

vols. Cairo: Matba'at al-madani.
TOEWS, JOHN E. 1987. "Intellectual History after the Linguistic Turn: The Autonomy of Meaning and the Irreducibility of Experience." *American Historical Review* 92, 4: 879–907.
TRITTON, ARTHUR S. 1930. *The Caliphs and Their Non-Muslim Subjects: A Critical Study of the Covenant of Umar.* London: Oxford University Press.
ULANSEY, DAVID. 1989. *The Origins of the Mithraic Mysteries: Cosmology and Salvation in the Ancient World.* New York: Oxford University Press.
UNVALA, JAMSHEDJI M., ed. and trans. 1921. *The Pahlavi Text "King Husrav and His Boy."* Paris: Paul Geuthner.
———. 1925. *Observations on the Religion of the Parthians.* Bombay: British India Press.
UNVALA, MANOCKJI R., ed. 1922. *Persian Revayats*, as *Darab Hormazyar's Rivayat*. 2 vols. Bombay: British India Press.
VAHMAN, FEREYDUN. 1985. "A Beautiful Girl." *Acta Iranica* 25, 665–674. Leiden: E. J. Brill.
———, ed. and trans. 1986. *Arda Wiraz Namag: The Iranian 'Divina Commedia.'* London: Curzon Press.
VANDEN BERGHE, LOUIS. 1959. *Archéologie de l'Iran ancien.* Leiden: E. J. Brill.
VAN HERIK, JUDITH. [1982] 1985. *Freud on Femininity and Faith.* Berkeley: University of California Press.
WAAG, ANATOL, ed. and trans. 1941. *Nirangistan, der Awestatraktat über die rituellen Vorschriften.* Leipzig: J. C. Hinrichs Verlag.
WAARDENBURG, JACQUES. [1973] 1999. *Classical Approaches to the Study of Religion: Aims, Methods and Theories of Research.* Berlin: Walter de Gruyter.
WACH, JOACHIM. 1988. *Introduction to the History of Religions.* Ed. J. M. Kitagawa and G. D. Alles. New York: Macmillan.
WARNER, ARTHUR G., AND EDMOND WARNER, trans. 1905–1925. *Shah nama*, by Abu 'l-Qasem Ferdowsi. 9 vols. London: Trübner.
WATERS, MATTHEW W. 1999. "The Earliest Persians in Southwestern Iran: The Textual Evidence." *Iranian Studies* 32, 1: 99–107.
WEBER, MAX. [1956] 1978. *Economy and Society: An Outline of Interpretive Sociology.* Ed. G. Roth and C. Wittich. 2 vols. Berkeley: University of California Press.
WENZEL, SIEGFRIED. 1968. "The Seven Deadly Sins: Some Problems of Research." *Speculum* 43, 1: 1–22.
WIDENGREN, GEO. 1983a. "La rencontre avec la daena, qui représente les

actions de l'homme." *Orientalia Romana* 5: 41–79.

———. 1983b. "Manichaeism and Its Iranian Background." In *The Cambridge History of Iran*. Vol. 3, 2, ed. E. Yarshater, 965–990. Cambridge: Cambridge University Press.

WIESEHÖFER, JOSEF. 1996. *Ancient Persia: From 550 BC to 650 AD*. London: I. B. Tauris.

WILLIAMS, ALLAN V. 1990a. "Bushasp." In *Encyclopaedia Iranica* 4, 568–569. London: Routledge and Kegan Paul.

———, ed. and trans. 1990b. *The Pahlavi Rivayat Accompanying the Dadestan i Denig*. 2 vols. Copenhagen: Munksgaard.

WINDFUHR, GERNOT L. 1976. "Vohu Manah: A Key to the Zoroastrian World-Formula." In *Michigan Oriental Studies in Honor of George G. Cameron*, ed. L. L. Orlin, 269–309. Ann Arbor: University of Michigan Department of Near Eastern Studies.

———. 1996. "The Logic of the Holy Immortals in Zoroastrianism." In *Proceedings of the Second North American Gatha Conference*, ed. S. J. H. Manekshaw and P. R. Ichaporia, 237–274. Womelsdorf, Pennsylvania: Federation of Zoroastrian Associations of North America.

———. 1999. "A Note on Aryaman's Social and Cosmic Setting." In *Aryan and Non-Aryan in South Asia: Evidence, Interpretation, and Ideology*, ed. J. Bronkhorst and M. M. Deshpande, 295–336. Cambridge, Massachusetts: Harvard University Department of Sanskrit and Indian Studies.

WRITER, RASHNA. 1994. *Contemporary Zoroastrians: An Unstructured Nation*. Lanham, Maryland: University Press of America.

YARSHATER, EHSAN, AND OTHERS, trans. 1985–1999. *Ta'rikh al-rusul wa 'l-muluk*, by Abu Ja'far Muhammad b. Jarir al-Tabari, as *The History of al-Tabari*. 39 vols. Albany: State University of New York Press.

YOUNG, SERINITY, ed. 1999. *Encyclopedia of Women and World Religion*. 2 vols. New York: Macmillan.

ZAEHNER, ROBERT C. 1961. *The Dawn and Twilight of Zoroastrianism*. London: Weidenfeld and Nicolson.

———. [1955] 1972. *Zurvan: A Zoroastrian Dilemma*. New York: Biblo and Tannen.

———. [1956] 1976. *The Teachings of the Magi: A Compendium of Zoroastrian Beliefs*. New York: Oxford University Press.

Zoroastrian College, Mazdayasnie Monasterie. 1990. Bombay: All India Shah Behram Baug Society.

Index

'Abbasids, 94, 99, 101
Abestag (Avesta), 13, 42
Abu Yusuf, 129–130
Achaemenians, 19, 46, 55, 75–81, 86, 127, 128
Adam, 52, 54, 126
Adur Anahid, 46
Adurbad, 40, 55
Afghanistan, 10
Ahuna Vairya (Ahunawar), 14
Ahura Mazda (Ohrmazd), 9, 10, 13, 16, 28, 45, 54, 57, 61, 62, 101, 115, 123, 128
    and Angra Mainyu, 18
    as a masculine entity, 28
    creation of Earth, 18
    creation of humans, 28–29
    creation of other spirits, 17
'A'isha, 130
Aka Manah (Akoman), 35, 36
Alexander, 81
'Ali b. Husayn, 96
Allah, 101
Allat, 83
Ameretat (Amurdad), 16, 45, 63
    as a neuter entity, 64
Amesha Spentas, 16–17, 63–64, 68
Amestris, 77
Amytis (Umaiti), 76, 77
Anatolia, 82, 83
Anaxshti, 36, 106
Angra Mainyu (Ahreman), 15, 17, 28, 54, 61, 115, 118, 119
    and Ahura Mazda, 18
    as a masculine entity, 28
    creation of other spirits, 17
Apama, 81
Aphrodite, 81
Apollo-Mithra-Helios, 83
Arab Muslims, 92–97
Arda Wiraz, 65
Arda Wiraz namag, 14, 65–71
Ardashir I, 84
Aredwi Sura Anahita (Ardwisur Anahid), 46–49, 71, 81, 82, 86, 87, 101, 125, 128–129, 130
Armenia, 83
    and Christianity, 57
    folk beliefs, 57
Artaxerxes II (Artaxshassa), 46, 55
Artaxerxes III, 81
Artaynte, 77
Artazostre (Artazaushtri), 76
Artemis (Diana), 46, 81, 83
Artemis-Anaitis, 82
Artystone (Rtastuna), 76, 78, 80, 91
Asha (Ard), 15
    and Drug, 31, 33
    neuter, 33
Asha Vahishta (Ardwahisht), 16, 45
Ashem Vohu, 14
Ashi, 41, 44, 49
aspanur (haspanwar), 86
Asrushti, 35–36, 68, 106
Astyages, 75
athravans, 13

Atossa (Utautha), 55, 76, 91
Avroman, 82
Azarmigduxt (Azarmeduxt), 85, 116
Azi (Az), 42–44, 106
Azi Dahaka, 126

Bactrian-Margiana Archeological
    Complex, 10, 52–53
Bag nask, 82
Baladhuri, al-, 93
Balkh, 95
Baluchistan, 128
Barashnum i no shab, 61
Bardiya (Smerdis), 76, 77
Barm-e Dilak, 84
Baykand (Paykand), 93
Black Sea, 92
Bombay, 24, 25, 26, 60, 108, 113
Boran, 85, 116
Bostanai, 101
British East India Company, 25
Buddhists, 46, 95
Bukhara, 94
Bundahishn, 33, 50, 124, 126
Bushyasta (Bushasp), 36, 37, 58, 106

Calcutta, 26
Cambyses II (Kambujiya), 76, 91, 129
Cassandane, 76
Central Asia, 22
Central Asian Bronze Age, 10
chador, 86
chagar wife, 97
Characene, 80
Chidag Handarz i Poryotkeshan, 54
childbirth, 47, 62, 91, 111, 113
Chinvato-Peretu (Chinwad Puhl), 20,
    68, 73
Christianity, 7, 86, 87, 96, 107, 109
    in Armenia, 57
    medieval, 50, 115–116, 117
clergy. *See* magi
consanguineous marriage, 77, 91, 129
conversion, 87, 94–98, 129
Cybele, 83
Cyrus (Kurush) the Younger, 55, 75
Cyrus II, 75–76, 78

Daena (Den), 20, 68, 70–73, 127
Daevas (Dews), 17, 73, 106, 118, 124
Daiwa (Dawi), 34, 106, 124
Dante, 14
Daqiqi, 40, 41
Darius I (Darayavahush), 32, 55, 57, 76,
    77, 78, 80, 124, 128
Darius II, 77
daxma, 23, 24
Delhi, 26
demonology, 2–3, 107, 118–119
Denag, 84
Denkard, 14, 34
Divine Comedy, 14
divorce, 90, 113, 131
dregvant (drvant), 32
Drug, 15, 31, 32, 34, 35, 48, 68, 105,
    106
    and Asha, 31, 33
    as a feminine personification of evil,
        32–33
    neuter, 33
Drvaspa (Druwasp), 44, 49
dualism, 1–2, 4, 6, 15–16
    and the feminine, 9–30
    decline of, 17–18, 107
    of good and evil, 2, 15–16, 37
Duzhyairya, 57, 106

Ebn Esfandiyar, 94
education and gender relations, 108–111,
    131
Elymais, 80
Emed i Ashawahishtan, 101, 129
emigration of Zoroastrians, 25, 26, 27,
    112
Eve, 52, 54, 126
evil, 1–3, 6, 15, 112, 115, 117, 119
    associations with, 1–2
    Drug, 31, 32–33
    origins of, 1–2
    perception of during the Middle
        Ages, 2

Fatima, 99, 130
Ferdowsi, Abu 'l-Qasem, 40
FEZANA Journal, 113

·INDEX·

fire temples, 22, 91, 95
fitna, 35, 40
Fravarane, 32, 132
fravashi, 116, 117, 124–125
Freftar, 124
Freni, 116
funerary towers, 23, 24

Gahanbars, 23
Gathas (Gah), 13, 14, 15, 31
Gayo-Maretan, 18, 39, 51
gazidag, 95
gender, 3
    implications in religion, 4, 5, 8, 115
    relationships within cultures, 5, 6–7
gender relations and education, 108–111
Ghazali, al-, 130
Golnar, 40
good, 1, 3, 15, 18, 119
Gordiya, 40
Gujarati language, 14, 122

Hadhoxt nask, 68
hagiography, 10–12, 87
Hamestagan, 20
Handarz i Oshnar, 56
Harahvaiti-Sarasvati, 46
Harun al-Rashid, 99
Hataria, Maneckji Limji, 111
Hatra, 83
Haurvatat (Hordad), 16, 45, 63
    as a neuter entity, 64
heaven, 14, 20, 65, 66, 67, 68, 71
hell, 14, 20, 65, 68
Hera, 81
Herbedestan, 91
Herodotus, 12, 75
hierodouleia, 83
Huris (Hur), 72
Husayn b. 'Ali, 96
Hutaosa, 116
Hvovi, 116

Ilkhanids, 103
Ilm-e Khshnum, 105
Iran, 9, 10, 22
Iranian theodicy, 1–2

Iranian tribal migrations, 122
Isfahan, 95
Ishtar, 46
Islam, 7, 94–102, 129
Istakhr, 46, 93
Izdundad, 101

Jahika (Jahi), 38–40, 48, 61, 93, 98, 106, 113
Jalula', 93
Jam, 126
    See also Yima
Jamaspa, 117, 130
Jamaspi (Jamaspig), 130
Jashan, 23
Jesus, 92
Jews, 96, 98, 99, 100, 101
jizya, 24, 27, 95
Judaism, 7

Karachi, 24, 60
Kem Na Mazda, 33, 62, 124
Khaltchayan, 83
Kirdir, 64

Lake Kayansih, 47
Los Angeles, 113

Madayan i Hazar Dadestan, 88
magavan, 12
magi, 12, 13, 91, 92, 93, 113
magu-paiti, 12
magus, 12
makush, 12
Malik b. Anas, 101
Mama, Arnavaz, 113
Mandane, 75, 76
Manichaeism, 42, 54, 72, 125, 127
Manthra Spenta (Maraspand), 37
Mardanfarrox, 126
Maria, 85, 86
marriage, 81, 90, 94, 96, 109, 112, 131
Martab (Maratib), 13
Mary the Harlot, 124
Mary Magdalene, 124
Mary the mother of Jesus, 49, 87
Mashya (Mahra), 50, 51–54, 107, 126

Mashyana (Mahriyana), 50, 51–54, 98, 107, 126
Master-Moos, Meher, 114
Mazda Ahura, 15, 118
Mazdaism. *See* Zoroastrianism
Mazda-worship. *See* Zoroastrianism
Mazdayasna (Mazdesn), 9
Mazdayasnie Monasterie, 113
Medes, 12
Meherjirana, Erachji, 105
menstruation, 61–62, 91, 111, 113, 130, 131
Merv al-Rud, 95
mihrab, 99
Mihragan, 23, 96
Mithra, 20, 44, 57, 96, 101, 118
Mithradata I (Mithradates), 82
Mithraism (Mysteries of Mithras), 56–57
mizhda, 73
Mongols, 103
mowbed, 12, 13, 50
mowmard, 12
Muhammad, 14, 35, 130
Musa, 82
Mush Parig, 57, 106
Muslims, 92–103
Mutawakkil, al-, 100

Nahn, 61
Nana (Nanaia), 81, 83
Naqsh-e Rostam, 78, 84
Narseh, 84
Narshakhi, al-, 93
nask, 82
Nasush, 59–63, 106, 113
Nav Ruz, 23, 96
Navar (Nawar), 13
Navjote, 21
Nerangestan, 91
New Persian language, 14, 122
Nezam al-Molk, 56
Nihavand, 95
Nike, 83

Old (Gathic) Avestan corpus, 4, 14, 122
Old Persian language, 77, 122
ossuary (*astodana*), 78

Otanes, 77

padixshay wife, 97
Padyab, 61
Pahlavi language, 14, 118, 122
Pahlavi, Mohammed Reza Shah, 112
Pahlavi, Reza Shah, 112
Pairika (Parig), 57–58, 63, 106
Pairimaiti (Parimati), 34, 106
Pakistan, 24, 108
Parthians, 19, 82–84, 86
Parysatis, 55, 77
Pasargadae, 78
Pelagia the Harlot, 124
Peroz, 25, 96
Persepolis Fortification Tablets, 75, 78, 79, 80
Persian Revayats, 15, 105, 106, 107
Phraataces V (Phraates), 82
Plato, 12
poll tax. *See gazidag, jizya*
pollution, 58–60, 91, 97–99, 100, 111, 113
polygyny, 77, 90, 111
Pouruchista, 116, 117
Pseudo-Smerdis (Gaumata), 76
Pythagoras, 12

Qabus nama, 41
Qajars, 111
Qazvin, 95
Quetta, 108

Radushdukka, 76
Radushnamuya, 76
Rashnu (Rashn), 20
Ray, 95
Rehbar-e Din-e Jarthushti, 15, 105, 106, 107
Rhodogune, 82
Rivetna, Roshan, 113
Roxane (Roxana), 81, 91
Rudaba, 40

Saddar Bondahesh, 72
Safavids, 103
Sakas (Scythians), 46

INDEX

Saoshyant (Soshans), 21
Sar Mashhad, 84
Sarakhs, 94
Sardis, 81
Sasanians, 19, 84–92, 107, 117, 129
Sedra-Pushun, 21
Seleucids, 81, 82
Seleucus I, 81
sexuality, 1, 3, 37–49, 87–88
Seyasat nama (Seyar al-moluk), 56
Shah nama, 40
Shah Pari, 130
Shahfarand (Shah i Afrid), 96
Shahrbanu, 96
Shahrokh, Farangis, 113
Shapur I, 84
Shapur II, 116
Shapurduxtag I, 84
Shapurduxtag II, 84
Sharifabad, 111
Shirin, 85, 86
Shkand Gumanig Wizar, 19–20
slavery, 75, 88, 93
Society for the Amelioration of the Conditions of the Zoroastrians in Persia, 111
Spanta Manyu (Spenta Mainyu), 15, 16, 123
Spenta Armaiti (Spendarmad), 16, 34–35, 44–45, 62, 81, 86, 87
Sraosha (Srosh), 20, 44, 62
Sri Gururani Nag Kanya (Nag Rani), 114
Sri Lanka, 24, 26, 108
Srosh Baj, 62
S's'andramata, 46
Sudaba, 40

Tabari, al-, 93, 130
Takrit, 95
Tarikh-i Bukhara, 93
Taromaiti (Taromati), 34, 106
Thea Urania, 82
theophoric names, 82
Thriti, 116
Timurids, 103
Tirmidhi, al-, 35

Tishtrya (Tishtar), 57
Tosar nama, 36
Tyche, 83

'Umar I, 93
'Umar II, 99
Umayyads, 99, 101
Uta (Udag), 44, 48, 90, 106

Vedic rites, 49
veiling, 86, 129
   See also chador
Verethraghna (Wahram), 44, 84
Videvdad (Widewdad), 14, 44
Vis, 40, 41, 56
Vis o Ramin, 40, 41, 56
Vishtaspa, 11, 116
Vohu Manah (Wahman), 16, 45

Wahram II, 84
Walid, al-, I, 96
witchcraft, 90
Wizidagiha i Zadspram, 32, 39, 42
women. *See* Zoroastrian women

Xerxes I (Xshayarsha), 55, 76, 77, 128
Xnathaiti, 44, 48, 106
Xshathra Vairya (Shahrewar), 16, 45, 106
Xusro ud Redag, 41, 56
Xusro I, 56, 87
Xusro II, 85–86
Xvarenah (Xwarrah), 42
xwedodah. See consanguineous marriage
Xwurdag Abestag (Khorde Avesta), 14

Yasna, 22
Yasna Haptanghaiti, 13–14, 16
Yazatas (Yazads), 17
Yazd, 27, 111
Yazdagird III, 25, 96
Yima (Jam, Jamshed), 33, 53, 73, 126
Yimi (Jamag), 53
Young (Standard) Avestan corpus, 14

Zadspram, 39
Zamyad Yasht, 126
Zand, 14, 117

Zand i Wahman Yasn, 19
Zarathushtra, 105, 115
    and Greek and Roman authors, 12
    birth of, 9–10, 19
    death of, 11
    hagiography of, 10–13
    on Asha and Drug, 15
Zarduxsht namag (Zardosht nama), 11
zaotars, 13
Zeus-Oromasdes, 83
Zoroaster, 9, 10
    See also Zarathushtra
Zoroastrian women
    and Christianity in the Sasanian period, 87, 92
    and the clergy (magi), 13, 113
    and diet, 100–101
    and divorce, 90, 113, 131
    and education, 108–111
    and Islam, 24, 96–99
    and leadership roles, 26, 76, 85–86, 113–114, 119
    and marriage, 90–91, 94, 109, 112
    and modern dress, 110
    and socioeconomic independence, 108
Zoroastrianism
    and Arab conquest, 93–94
    and blood, 61–62
    and childbirth, 62
    and death, 20
    and education, 108–109
    and female demons, 3–4, 105–107, 118–119
    and Muslims, 24–25, 96–99
    and pollution, 58–59
        two major categories of, 59–60
    and polygyny, 77, 90, 111
    and Protestant Christianity, 17, 107
    and the status of women, 5–6, 44, 108, 110–111, 113–120
    concept of heaven, hell, and limbo, 20–21
    cosmogony, 18–19
    demonology, 1–2, 6–7, 17, 119–120
    eschatology, 21
    funerary rites, 23–24
    history of, 9–13, 18–19, 24–28
    initiation into, 21–22
    loss of political authority, 25, 102
    method of overcoming evil, 19–20
    notion of the feminine, 2–3, 6–7, 115–116, 119–120
    origins of, 3–4, 9–10
    perceptions of good and evil, 1–3, 15–16, 17–18
        historical development of, 1–2
    scriptures, 13–14
    sex and sexuality, 1, 3, 37–49, 87–88
    spirituality and gender, 2
    system of dualism, 29–30
    See also Zarathushtra
Zoroastrians (Mazdeans)
    and conversion, 24, 87, 94–98, 129
    and education, 108–111
    and intermarriage, 112
    and orthodoxy, 113–114, 120
    and secularization, 27, 108, 109, 110, 111
    and westernization, 25–26, 107, 109
    in Australia, 26
    in Canada, 26
    in the Caucasus, 25
    in China, 25
    in England, 26
    in the United States of America, 26
    Iranian, 3–5, 9, 18, 24, 120
    Parsis, 3–5, 9, 18, 24, 120
    women
        and Christianity, 87, 92
        and clergy, 13, 113
        and diet, 100–101
        and education, 108–111
        and divorce, 90, 113, 131
        and Islam, 24, 96–99
        and leadership roles, 26, 76, 85–86, 113–114, 119
        and marriage, 90–91, 94, 109, 112
        and modern dress, 110
        and socioeconomic independence, 108
Zurvanism, 16, 42

TORONTO STUDIES IN RELIGION

Donald Wiebe, General Editor

This series of monographs is designed as a contribution to the scholarly and academic understanding of religion. Such understanding is taken to involve both a descriptive and an explanatory task. The first task is conceived as one of surface description involving the gathering of information about religions, and depth description that provides, on the basis of the data gathered, a more finely nuanced description of a tradition's self-understanding. The second task concerns the search for explanation and the development of theory to account for religion and for particular historical traditions. The series, furthermore, covers the phenomenon of religion in all its constituent dimensions and geographic diversity. Both established and younger scholars in the field have been and will be included to represent a wide range of viewpoints and positions, producing original work of high order at the monograph and major study level.

Although predominantly empirically oriented, the series encourages theoretical studies and even leaves room for creative and empirically controlled philosophical and speculative approaches in the interpretation of religions and religion. Toronto Studies in Religion is of particular interest to those who study the subject at universities and colleges but is also of value to the general educated reader.

For additional information about this series or for the submission of manuscripts, please contact:

Peter Lang Publishing, Inc.
Acquisitions Department
P.O. Box 1246
Bel Air, Maryland 20104-1246

To order other books in this series, please contact our Customer Service Department:

(800) 770-LANG (within the U.S.)
(212) 647-7706 (outside the U.S.)
(212) 647-7707 FAX

or browse online by series at:
WWW.PETERLANGUSA.COM